BOURDIEU
for EDUCATORS

SAGE was founded in 1965 by Sara Miller McCune to support the dissemination of usable knowledge by publishing innovative and high-quality research and teaching content. Today, we publish more than 750 journals, including those of more than 300 learned societies, more than 800 new books per year, and a growing range of library products including archives, data, case studies, reports, conference highlights, and video. SAGE remains majority-owned by our founder, and after Sara's lifetime will become owned by a charitable trust that secures our continued independence.

Los Angeles | London | Washington DC | New Delhi | Singapore | Boston

BOURDIEU for EDUCATORS

Policy and Practice

Fenwick W. English
The University of North Carolina at Chapel Hill

Cheryl L. Bolton
Staffordshire University

Los Angeles | London | New Delhi
Singapore | Washington DC | Boston

Los Angeles | London | New Delhi
Singapore | Washington DC | Boston

FOR INFORMATION:

SAGE Publications, Inc.

2455 Teller Road

Thousand Oaks, California 91320

E-mail: order@sagepub.com

SAGE Publications Ltd.

1 Oliver's Yard

55 City Road

London EC1Y 1SP

United Kingdom

SAGE Publications India Pvt. Ltd.

B 1/I 1 Mohan Cooperative Industrial Area

Mathura Road, New Delhi 110 044

India

SAGE Publications Asia-Pacific Pte. Ltd.

3 Church Street

#10-04 Samsung Hub

Singapore 049483

Printed in the United States of America

A catalog record of this book is available from the Library of Congress.

ISBN 978-1-4129-9659-4 (P)

This book is printed on acid-free paper.

Acquisitions Editor: Theresa Accomazzo

Editorial Assistant: Georgia McLaughlin

Production Editor: Nicola Marshall

Copy Editor: Megan Granger

Typesetter: C&M Digitals (P) Ltd.

Proofreader: Susan Schon

Indexer: Author

Cover Designer: Scott Van Atta

Marketing Manager: Terra Schultz

Brief Contents

Preface   xi

About the Authors   xv

1. Introducing Pierre Bourdieu to the Practitioner   1

2. Unmasking the School Asymmetry and the Social System   25

3. The Curriculum, Qualifications, and Life Chances   53

4. The Shifting Control of Leadership Preparation   77

5. A Retrospective Look at Bourdieu's Impact   103

References   111

Index   123

Detailed Contents

Preface   xi

About the Authors   xv

1. Introducing Pierre Bourdieu to the Practitioner   1

What This Chapter Is About   1

Introduction   2

Bourdieu's Biography   3

Vielseitigkeit: What Is Distinctive About Bourdieu   7

Understanding the Nature of Pedagogic
    Work as Political Struggle   8

The "Culture Wars" in the United States and
    United Kingdom: Similarities and Differences   10

The Battle Over the Correct Academic Subjects and
    Proper Pedagogic Work   12

The Concept of Misrecognition and How It Works   14

Some History With Misrecognition   15

Building Awareness of the Forces at Play   18

Without New Eyes: The Blinders of Doxa as Orthodoxy   19

Bourdieu as the Public Intellectual, Activist,
    and Provocateur   20

Implications for Policy and Practice   21

    A Social World of Policy and Practice That
        Is Dynamic, Fluid, and Contested   21

    Repressive and Discriminatory Educational Practices
        Persist Because Even Those Who Are Disadvantaged by
        Them Accept Them as "Legitimate"   22

    School Practitioners Are Part of the Problem if
        They Don't See How Schools Really Work 22

Key Chapter Concepts   23

2. Unmasking the School Asymmetry and the Social System   **25**

What This Chapter Is About   25
Introduction   26
Bourdieusian Cornerstones   27
Bourdieu's Concept of Habitus   28
An Example of Neighborhood Habitus   29
A Case Study of How Family Habitus Works to
    Shape Career Aspirations   30
The Intersection of Class and Social Space/Field   31
An Example of a Field With Its Own Logic   33
The Cultural Arbitrary   35
The Plight of Minority Children Facing the
    Dominant Cultural Arbitrary in Schools   36
How the System Works as a Game   39
Who Benefits From Schools as They Are?   41
Illusio and Unquestioned Loyalty to Continuing
    Orthodoxies   42
The Bounded Nature of Choice Within a
    Designated Social Space   43
Educational Inequalities Must Remain Unnamed   45
Connecting the Dots: The Importance of Family in
    School Success   46
The Challenge of Reducing Social Inequality as an
    Educational Goal   48
Implications for Policy and Practice   49
Key Chapter Concepts   49

3. The Curriculum, Qualifications, and Life Chances   **53**

What This Chapter Is About   53
Introduction   55
The Three Forms of Capital   55
Empirical Validation of the Impact of Social Capital
    on School Success   56
The Power of Cultural Capital and Bourdieu's
    Own Experience as a Student   57
Schools as Institutionalized Embodiments of Forms
    of Cultural Capital   58
Capital, Power, Symbolic Violence, and
    Scholastic Habitus   59
Two Recent Examples of Symbolic Power (Violence)
    in School Curricula   60

Social Origin and School Success: Historical and
 Continuing Evidence of the Linkage Between Them   62
Academic Failure as the "Fault" of the Student?   64
Academic Credentials—Essential Capital?   65
The Hidden Curriculum, Cultural Values,
 and School Success   67
Calculating Life Chances: The Academic
 Versus Vocational Education Debate   68
The Maldistribution of Opportunity   70
Implications for Policy and Practice   72
Key Chapter Concepts   73

4. The Shifting Control of Leadership Preparation   **77**

What This Chapter Is About   77
Introduction   79
The Construction of National Leadership Standards
 in the United Kingdom and United States   80
The Major Epistemological Steps Behind
 National Standards   81
Core Technologies and the Reification of the
 Status Quo   84
The Shifting Nature of the Contestation and
 Change in Power in the Educational Field   84
A Hard Look Back: A Trajectory of Class Control
 of Schools and Education   92
The Decontextualization of School Leaders
 via Job Standardization   95
The Reformers' Blinkered Vision for Change:
 They Just Don't See It   96
Implications for Policy and Practice   97
  Ideologies and the Interrelational World of Educational
   Policy and Practice   97
  Educational Leadership Preparation Remains in a
   Confused and Contested State   98
  The Battle for the Dominant Ideology of School
   Leadership Continues   99
Key Chapter Concepts   100

5. A Retrospective Look at Bourdieu's Impact   **103**

What This Chapter Is About   103
Introduction   104

The Social Field of Education Is Not Static   104
Education Is Simultaneously a Means and an End   105
Schooling as the Cultural Arbitrary Demonizes
    Those Who Are "Otherized"   106
The Dominant Consumer Culture in Education
    Undermines Its Moral and Humanistic Value   107
Educational Reform Will Always Benefit and
    Advantage the Reformers   107
The Dilemma of School Leadership: Agent of the
    State or of Humanity?   108
Implications for Policy and Practice   108
    Can the Logic of Practice Be Changed?   108
Key Chapter Concepts   110

References   **111**
Index   **123**

Preface

This is a book for educational practitioners and policymakers who work anyplace in the world where there is a state-supported public educational system. Pierre Bourdieu produced an extensive range of works in many different fields, but a good number of them were focused on education. While he was a French philosopher–sociologist–researcher and public activist for popular and democratic causes in a particular time and culture, his insights, understandings, and humanity created a corpus of provocative books, articles, and commentaries that continue to strike chords of commonality across cultures and nations, keeping his ideas vibrant and relevant today.

Our purpose in writing this book is to bring Bourdieu's principal educational ideas and insights to a wider audience of educators than those typically found in purely academic institutions of higher education. An excellent sample of books and anthologies about Bourdieu exists in sociology and other disciplines; however, this book has been specifically developed for the largest group of educators working in the schools of the world: those who lead for learning in the primary, elementary, and secondary institutions where the bulk of children attend.

While we did not assume that our readers were deeply read in sociology, philosophy, or any specific academic discipline, we did expect that Bourdieu's name would at least be tangentially familiar to them, even if they had not read widely about him or his ideas. We also assumed that our readers were very familiar with the issues nearly all schools in the world face: how to educate children of all backgrounds effectively, how to confront socioeconomic disparity and poverty, and how to create more socially just societies.

Our exposition and explanation of Bourdieu's writing represent the most important concepts of what he offered to the world of policy and practice, at least as we understand them as practitioners in those worlds. This was no easy task, as much of Bourdieu's academic writing was directed to sociologists and researchers who would be intimately familiar with his references and concepts. Our presentation tries to avoid arcane and highly technical issues that would require such specialized knowledge.

A further element of complexity in accessing Bourdieu's work is that he created his own vocabulary in which to locate his ideas. He did this because he believed that ordinary words from common use were too slippery to carry the special connotations and meanings he saw as necessary to attain any new insights or understandings about what and how schools actually work. This special vocabulary can be initially off-putting, but we have attempted to ease the reader into it gradually and to explain the various concepts with reference to current educational events. Our sequencing of his concepts is therefore a matter of our choice in bringing the reader into Bourdieu's world.

We do not claim to have included all Bourdieu's works or ideas—only those that we believed, based on our own experiences, would help those working in schools understand some of the larger social and political issues affecting them. Our criteria for deciding what to address in this book were therefore a rough kind of practical rubric for inclusion or exclusion. While we have provided examples of current situations to illustrate some possible applications of Bourdieu's concepts, we have not set out to engage in speculation about what Bourdieu would do or think, beyond what he wrote and beyond informed scholarly opinion of his writings and researches.

Finally, we want to communicate to our readers that, as sociologist Richard Jenkins (2002) once wrote of Bourdieu, he was "enormously stimulating" and was "good to think with" (p. 176). Michael Grenfell (2004) called Bourdieu an "agent provocateur." We are confident that as you take this journey of learning about him with us, you will also agree with their assessments. We think you will discover in Bourdieu a fascinating, complex, insightful philosopher–social scientist who once wrote, "My principle has always been to say what is hardest for my audience to swallow—the very opposite of demagogy" (Bourdieu, 2008, pp. 49–50).

If you care about education and children, equity, diversity, and social justice, you will find in Bourdieu a relentless critic of schooling everywhere. But equally present in his pursuit of piecing together the creation and use of social and economic power is a way toward equity, diversity, and social justice not previously perceived on a wide scale among educators or policy developers.

With patience and persistence, we believe that by using Bourdieu's work we can arrive at a new vision or a metanoia about what it will really take to reform schools so they become more successful with all students and, as a result, more socially just places for every society. That the educational reforms proffered by politicians in both our countries have thus far failed to deliver on their promises is not surprising. Bourdieu explains why, and for this reason alone we believe he is worth the effort to understand. We hope that this book for educational practitioners will start the journey toward such an understanding.

Fenwick W. English, Chapel Hill, North Carolina

Cheryl L. Bolton, Staffordshire, United Kingdom

About the Authors

Fenwick W. English (PhD, Arizona State University) is the R. Wendell Eaves Senior Distinguished Professor of Educational Leadership in the School of Education at the University of North Carolina at Chapel Hill, a position he has held since 2001. A practitioner turned scholar, Dr. English has been a school principal, assistant superintendent, and superintendent of schools in elementary/secondary education in California, Florida, and New York. He has served in Ohio and Indiana as a department chair, dean, and vice chancellor of academic affairs in higher education. He is the author or coauthor of more than 35 books spanning a period of more than 40 years. He served as president of the University Council of Educational Administration in 2006–2007 and as president of the National Council of Professors of Educational Administration (NCPEA) in 2011–2012. In 2013, he received the Living Legend Award from NCPEA for his lifetime contribution to the field of educational leadership. He and Dr. Cheryl L. Bolton have presented their research papers at meetings of the American Educational Research Association and the British Educational Leadership, Management, and Administration Society for the past 5 years.

Cheryl L. Bolton (PhD, Staffordshire University) is responsible for a range of education programs, including education doctorates and wider professional development for teachers and others in education. She worked in industry before moving to education, becoming a teacher in college, developing teacher education programs, and moving to Staffordshire University in 2008, where she has continued to work with educators of learners of all ages and across different establishments. Dr. Bolton has written a number of publications relating to educational leadership, which have appeared in *The Journal of Educational Administration* and *Journal of School Leadership*, and a chapter on the work of Pierre Bourdieu and Basil Bernstein in the 2011 *SAGE Handbook of Educational Leadership* (second edition). She has presented papers at meetings of the American Educational Research Association and the British Educational Research Association in the United Kingdom.

1

Introducing Pierre Bourdieu to the Practitioner

WHAT THIS CHAPTER IS ABOUT

The name Pierre Bourdieu may not be familiar to many educational practitioners in public school settings in the United States, the United Kingdom, or anywhere else. This introductory chapter is aimed at acquainting the school-practitioner reader (teacher, administrator, counselor, social worker) with a general appraisal of Bourdieu and why his stature continues to grow internationally. It also is an attempt to indicate why Bourdieu's ideas, research, and thought are powerful, insightful, and useful despite being somewhat difficult to understand initially.

Specifically, this chapter addresses the following points:

- Bourdieu's concept of a social space as contested presents a fluid and dynamic model of contestation in education, along with the notion of misrecognition.

- Bourdieu's unique vocabulary for concepts presents an initial dilemma in coming to a quick and easy understanding of his work.

- Bourdieu's concepts and ideas have to be seen not in the usual linear fashion (A, B, C, etc.) but as an integrated whole that does not depend on unequivocal categorical definitional boundaries.

Ideas are defined not by themselves but in relation to other ideas. Readers accustomed to conceptual singularity and stand-alone definitions may find this feature of Bourdieu's body of work off-putting at first. We will work hard to ease this transition and any potential tension it creates.

INTRODUCTION

Educational practitioners may not know Bourdieu because the world of classroom and administrative practice was not one in which he traveled, wrote, or researched. He penned no popular works on how to improve schools or teaching. For most of his career, Bourdieu was a sequestered academic in a prestigious French university, where he pursued his research interests in sociology.

Even among fellow academics, Bourdieu was somewhat of an eccentric. He was a trenchant critic of the French educational system for its failure to live up to its Republican aims (Lane, 2006). In this respect, his criticisms have great appeal and relevance to other educational systems in other countries that are anchored in a universal approach to education irrespective of class and/or wealth and yet consistently produce results that privilege and reinforce class and wealth.

The disparity between educational goals and educational results so readily observable in the United States, United Kingdom, Canada, Australia, and other nations is not produced by a failure of political aims or even funding. Huge monetary sums, public and private, have been allocated in the United States and elsewhere to eliminate disparities in promoting educational achievement that are rooted in race, class, and social position. But Bourdieu's work cuts through the political rhetoric and exposes the interests of those who control public education, showing how their selection of reforms is designed to maintain their dominant position in determining what schools do to reinforce and perpetuate social inequality.

In short, Bourdieu's work exposes the contradiction behind the mask of democratic and meritocratic goals and reforms, and shows why none of them will likely erase the achievement gaps and other discrepancies that currently exist in educational systems. It isn't that the public educational system can't be reformed; rather, it is unlikely to be reformed under any of the proposed political approaches currently being debated in the popular public and policy circles, and especially not with approaches centered on school choice and privatization (the neoliberal agenda Bourdieu vehemently fought against as a public intellectual in the latter part of his life). These popular approaches are not designed to confront social inequalities that emerging research strongly suggests are at the root of the gaps in school achievement (Condron, 2011; Sahlberg, 2011). In the end, they only serve to perpetuate these inequalities.

Bourdieu's work, conducted over an extended time period, helps in reexamining the nature of public schooling everywhere. His dogged pursuit of how public schools continue to fail the public is what ultimately makes him worth reading, to help school leaders and teachers understand more accurately how the work they do in the schools will or will not transform them into more democratic and truly meritocratic institutions. The true nature of Bourdieu's work rests on his understanding of the forms of cultural power and domination (see Lebaron, 2010). This is the work that has propelled Bourdieu into the international fame on which his reputation rests today.

Bourdieu (1990b) believed that by using the instruments of sociology he could discern the mental categories and structures teachers used in schools and, by so doing, could reveal the social dichotomies and disparities that educational systems teach (see also Savage & English, 2013). He professed that "sociology unmasks self-deception, that collectively entertained and encouraged form of lying to oneself which, in every society, is at the basis of the most sacred values and, thereby, of all social existence" (Bourdieu, 1990b, p. 188). Bourdieu's life in the academy, his humble beginnings as a student of the lower classes, and his belief in the power of self-criticism, even as it contained blind spots he himself was not always able to discern, all provide lessons for those who desire a more broadly based avenue for humanistic education in public schools everywhere.

BOURDIEU'S BIOGRAPHY

Bourdieu (2004b) was a firm advocate of reflexive approaches, acutely aware of how his own experiences influenced his thinking; yet he was contemptuous of biography as a method of discerning truth. He wrote about himself as a critique of his life and work, and underscored that this remembrance was not a biography. As a result of his avoidance of traditional biography, there is not a lot of intimate, personal data about him beyond a kind of general outline of his 72 years of life (1930–2002).

Bourdieu was born in 1930 in a small village in the French Pyrenees. His family was of modest means, and the particular French dialect he spoke is no longer considered a living variation of the language today. He was sent to a boarding school and exhibited superior academic ability, though aspects of his boarding school experience were filled with the usual form of torment and bullying from other boys. He completed his secondary education in Paris and graduated from the École Normale Supérieure in 1955 with a degree in philosophy.

Although Bourdieu would rise to the heights of the French university system, he always had some ambivalence toward it. He railed against the conformity of the university and found himself confronting an intellectual world that believed itself to be liberated and open-minded but that he found to be profoundly conservative and conformist. This insight moved him to comment, "I have almost always found myself on the opposite side from the models and modes dominant in the field" (Bourdieu, 2004b, p. 106).

Bourdieu's failure to submit his doctoral thesis was part and parcel of his refusal to play the university game and submit to its rules. Later, he consoled himself with a line from Kafka, which counseled, "Do not present yourself before a court whose verdict you do not recognize" (Bourdieu, 2004b, p. 101).

One of the defining moments in his life was being sent to Algeria during the war for Algerian independence from France. The terror and brutality of that colonial conflict changed his outlook on his life's work. France invaded Algeria, a state of some 919,500 square miles in northwest Africa, in 1830 and made it a French colony in 1848. Subsequently, thousands of Europeans migrated to Algeria and settled there, subjecting the local Sunni Muslim population to European culture and power. The European population confiscated land and set themselves up to be the arbiters of all matters, over the local inhabitants. However, a war for independence broke out in 1954. After 7 years of protracted and bitter fighting, during which "at least 100,000 Muslims and 10,000 French soldiers were killed, Algeria became independent in 1962" (Lagasse, 1994, p. 21).

Bourdieu went to Algeria to finish out his military service in 1955 (Grenfell, 2007, p. 13). There, he was witness to extreme violence and bloodshed in which "the scale of reprisals and torture carried out by the French paratroopers shocked the nation" (p. 38). Bourdieu (2004b) recalls that he refused to enter the reserve officers' college because he "could not bear the idea of dissociating [himself] from the rank-and-file soldiers" and because he found that he shared little in common with the candidates for officer (p. 37).

On the ship that took him to Algeria, he wrote that he tried in vain to ask the soldiers, "illiterates from the whole of western

France" (Bourdieu, 2004b, p. 95), tough questions about going to war. He confessed that he tried to stir in them "the need to revolt against the absurd 'pacification' which [they] were being sent to assist" (p. 95), but he made little headway as they replied, "You'll get us all killed" (p. 95).

Despite the country being in upheaval because of the war, Bourdieu carried out extensive sociological studies of Algerian society with the idea of showing "the extent to which French colonialism had destroyed it" (Grenfell, 2004, p. 39). He studied the four major groups that formed non-European Algerian society: the Kabyles, the Shawia, the Mozabites, and the Arab-speaking peoples. He contrasted traditional social norms with modern norms, especially highlighting the differences in gender roles in the traditional societies. He wrote several books about his experiences in Algeria, particularly important among them being *The Logic of Practice* (1980/1990a).

This period of time was important to Bourdieu. He was totally engaged in his sociological studies, and he believed that his intensity of effort was "rooted . . . in the extreme sadness and anxiety in which [he] lived" (Bourdieu, 2004b, p. 47). Thinking back on his time in Algeria, Bourdieu confessed that it involved a "transformation of [his] vision of the world" (p. 58) and that his personal motivation there was prompted by his need "to overcome [his] guilty conscience about merely being a participant observer in this appalling war" (Honneth, Kocyba, & Schwibs, 1986, p. 44).

From an educational standpoint, Algeria was a pivotal time for Bourdieu because his ethnographic studies of Algerian society showed him the power of education to change traditional modes of thinking and acting. He understood why the traditional community of Algerian elders resisted education: They correctly perceived the threat it posed to their native ways of thinking and their own positions of authority in their communities.

Bourdieu also began to map out a social class taxonomy of Algerian society and to examine how larger societal changes impacted various class levels and the people within them. His explanation of change was at odds with the views of others, including "intellectuals with Marxist sympathies" (Grenfell, 2007, p. 72).

A key insight was that the group of people in Algerian society, or any society for that matter, who had economic security and stability also had the capability to forward-project time into a state that did not exist (i.e., what we would call *the future*). People that had no such material conditions had no such capacity. In short, they could not consider a *future* at all.

According to Grenfell (2007), Bourdieu also tried to reconcile the competing demands and contradictions of modern society and its need for education. As he worked in this area, he rejected a "highly centralized, top-down driven education agenda" (p. 74). In its place, he considered the possibility of a different approach in which the individual and the larger social structure might be harmonized.

It was in Algeria that Bourdieu began to construct a vision that would connect individuals "with the social structures that surrounded them and the personal cognitive structures which guided their thoughts and actions" (Grenfell, 2007, p. 75). When he left Algeria to return to France, "education became his prime focus of work" (p. 75).

Bourdieu returned to France in 1960 and became a graduate assistant to Raymond Aron, a leading French philosopher of the period who was connected to an inner circle of top-ranked academics such as Jean-Paul Sartre (Collins, 1998, p. 775). He did some university teaching and was named the director of the Center for European Sociology, where he wrote two important books in education: *Reproduction in Education, Society, and Culture* with Jean-Claude Passeron (1970/2000) and *Outline of a Theory of Practice* (1972/1977).

His work with Passeron was a landmark book and has gone through numerous reprintings since it was first released. Grenfell (2007) claims "it is this book, more than any other, which establishes Bourdieu's reputation and it is still among the most-cited of his works" (p. 94).

Bourdieu (1990b) characterized his academic work by reflecting, "For me, intellectual life is closer to the artist's life than to the routines of academic life" (p. 26). While Bourdieu remained in the broad sociological traditions of inquiry for most of his academic career, he was not afraid to cross over into other fields if he believed it was necessary. He was thus a border crosser, and his writing has to be seen as representing his determination not to be confined or defined within a neat academic box. He spoke out on what moved him, and he used a wide variety of public forums to do so, from popular magazines to the usual, more esoteric academic journals read by very few politicians and pundits. Bourdieu was that rare academic who was comfortable tackling controversies in the more mainline avenues of public discourse. He also incurred academic criticism from his colleagues for these public forays. The translation from academic discourse to more mainline venues is replete with the dangers of overstatement and easy generalization. Bourdieu accepted this danger and appeared not to be unduly concerned about it.

VIELSEITIGKEIT: WHAT IS DISTINCTIVE ABOUT BOURDIEU

Several distinctive aspects of Bourdieu's work have to be understood to come to grips with the power of his ideas. First, Bourdieu pursued his work as a practicing sociologist. He was interested in working to understand and resolve certain issues within sociology. He was not first and foremost a theorist; theory was a practical means to help him resolve problems he encountered in his field studies. He believed in working from the ground up—that is, dealing with real issues in context and backing into theory to bring coherence to his work.

Bourdieu's work is also evolutionary. He was constantly reappraising and recentering key concepts. Bourdieu also brought to his work a special vocabulary to define his major concepts and lines of intellectual development. The purpose of that vocabulary was to avoid having to dispel all the numerous layers of meaning that come with familiar terms. By using newly invented words he could attach his own meanings, and he could also connect them in a way that suited his ideas regarding their application. As Swartz (1997) notes, Bourdieu believed that "the experience of familiarity . . . stands as one of the principal obstacles to a scientific understanding of the social world"; so in his work he "self-consciously selects terminology and cultivates a writing style that establishes distance from everyday language use" (p. 13).

Bourdieu's concepts are relational and interactive. This feature of Bourdieu's work presents some formidable obstacles in coming to understand him. Definitions are not categorically clean and often appear vague, and where they are provided they may seem inconsistent. Readers of conventional research and self-help books on leadership who expect precision in categorical clarity are likely to be frustrated. In Bourdieu's work, he refused simple answers because, in the end, they are not very helpful in actually changing things.

Bourdieu's focus was on, for lack of a better term, "the big picture" of social interaction and how various aspects influenced other aspects. Bourdieu (1990b) described his perspective by recalling the concept of *vielseitigkeit,* a German term from Max Weber that referred to "the many-sidedness of social reality" (p. 21). It was this "manysidedness" that was most important, and how the various features work with one another is what makes Bourdieu both difficult and enlightening at the same time. Bourdieu (1990b) himself described his view as comprising the "tensions, oppositions, the relations of power which constitute the structure of a field or of the social field as a totality at any given point in time" (p. 118).

This feature of Bourdieu's approach represents a major intellectual and conceptual difference from the work of many others. As such, the use of a special vocabulary coupled with a dynamic and fluid conceptual base means that Bourdieu's corpus is of another kind altogether. Because Bourdieu was more interested in problem solving than creating a major theoretical apparatus, his work appears disjointed and conceptually jagged at times, and piecing together his principal lines of thought has to be done over many books, articles, and compendia that stretch across his entire academic and public career.

Perhaps the most appropriate characterization of Bourdieu's refusal to employ "ordinary language" was that he wanted to remind his reader that what he was constructing was an account of reality and not reality itself. Or as Jenkins (2002) observed, "He [Bourdieu] is trying to prevent the 'reality of the model' becoming confused with the 'model of reality'" (p. 169). For this reason, the reader must be patient as Bourdieu's thinking is unfolded and explained in this book.

UNDERSTANDING THE NATURE OF PEDAGOGIC WORK AS POLITICAL STRUGGLE

The educational practitioner normally works within a set of bureaucratic agencies, each with a set of rules and expectations. Usually via policy directive or a law, new actions are defined within a context of expectations and requirements. The requirements may also be accompanied by a definition of rewards and sanctions. The embodied actions are then given to a set of agencies and institutions for implementation in the schools, and school-based practitioners engage in the work itself. Many practitioners never even think about the larger socio political arena in which they toil day in and day out, believing that if they just do their work, the politics of the moment will leave them alone. Unfortunately, the increasing intrusiveness of political change should have convinced even the most naïve that this view of education is a thing of the past, if it ever existed at all. In some U.S. states, teacher tenure laws have been abolished. The linkage between obtaining a master's degree and increased salary advancement has been erased. Teacher collective bargaining agreements have been abrogated and teacher due process procedures severely limited. Teacher evaluations now must include student test score gains, and in some jurisdictions teachers who fail to demonstrate improvement may have their license to practice revoked. These changes are not random acts but a well-coordinated and well-funded effort to change the nature of the control of public education in the United States (see English, 2014).

Bourdieu's sociological analyses of how power and domination are attained in various fields, including education, would have predicted how various groups within a field can come to impose their vision of the world through the use of multiple forms of capital. That would include the powerful billionaires such as Bill Gates and Eli Broad who are pushing a variety of "reforms" for public schools, and how neoconservative think tanks such as the Heritage Foundation and the American Enterprise Institute combine with the U.S. Department of Education to compel adherence to their agenda in the Race to the Top federal initiative (see Ravitch, 2010b).

If there is a silver lining to Bourdieu's analyses of power and domination, it is this:

> In the struggle for the production and imposition of a legitimate vision of the social world, the holders of bureaucratic authority never obtain an absolute monopoly, even when they add the authority of science, as do state economists, to their bureaucratic authority. (Bourdieu, 1990b, p. 137)

This means that realignment is possible as contrary individuals, agents, and agencies engage in a struggle to converge around a different agenda. This picture of competition is Bourdieu's insight into political struggle as one of attaining legitimacy and hence hegemony in the education field. Bourdieu said it like this: "Legitimacy is indivisible: there is no agency to legitimate the legitimacy" (Bourdieu & Passeron, 1970/2000, p. 18). This is especially the case in U.S. education, where there is no equivalent of a national ministry of education and no culture akin to many European and/or Asian nations. The decentralization of U.S. education to the 50 states ensures consistent competition for influence within and across the states.

Bourdieu uses the word *pedagogy* not in the usual sense of "the science, principles, or work of teaching" (Higgleton, Sargeant, & Seaton, 1999, p. 657) but, rather, in the sense of a critical reading and even deconstruction of the pedagogical relationship that is rooted in a parent/child (hierarchical) dyad. In Bourdieu's terminology (see Bourdieu & Passeron, 1970/2000) the actions are called *pedagogic actions*. The agencies and/or institutions involved receive *pedagogic authority* to implement the *pedagogic actions.* These result in practitioners' engaging in *pedagogic work.* This relationship is shown in Figure 1.1.

Figure 1.1   Bourdieu's Relational Field of Educational Interests

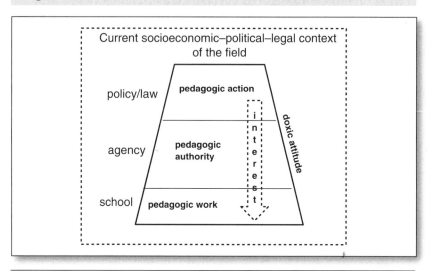

Source: Pierre Bourdieu and Jean-Claude Passeron (2000) *Reproduction in Education, Society and Culture* (2nd ed.) London: SAGE.

The arena of *pedagogic action* is the larger social space where individuals, agents, agencies, and groups engage in a contest to impose their version of how the world should work. Such interests are either in favor of preserving the status quo or in favor of transforming it. And in the continuing battle of linguistic symbols, agents claiming to "reform" education may actually be working to dominate all forms of education with a simple economic calculus where the mentality of profit, customers, and consumerism eclipses the ethic of public service.

THE "CULTURE WARS" IN THE UNITED STATES AND UNITED KINGDOM: SIMILARITIES AND DIFFERENCES

The current struggle for what has been called "the soul of public education" is at least 40 years old in the United States and a bit younger in the United Kingdom. In the United States, this struggle was formerly known as "the culture wars" (Shor, 1986). One of the very first manifestations of cultural conflict that spilled over into education occurred over the teaching of Darwin's theory of evolution. While very few in the scientific community take issue with this narrative, its premises are hotly disputed by the nonscientific community as represented in local school boards, state boards of education, state legislatures, and even Congress in the United States (Smith, Heinscke, & Jarvis, 2004).

Even as evolution was thought by some to have been resolved in the infamous Scopes trial in Tennessee in 1925 (Bates, 1993), more than 80 years later the chairman of the Texas State Board of Education declared, "Evolution is hooey" (Collins, 2012, p. 18). Eugenie Scott, executive director of the National Center for Science Education, lamented that evolution is "settled science" and "we shouldn't fight the culture wars in the high school classroom" (Tracy, 2012, p. A6).

The issue of climate change has now become the flashpoint in the continuing battles over which culture will be taught in schools, once again pitting "settled science" against popular nonscientific advocates who happen to be on school boards or in state legislatures. A local school board member in Colorado worked to prevent teachers in her school district from teaching climate change as a fact, remarking, "Unless we've got conclusive evidence one way or another—and I don't think we'll have that for hundreds of years—I think both sides should be taught. Allow the kids to figure it out for themselves" (Tracy, 2012, p. A6). The director of the National Research Council retorted, "What would be conveyed to them [the kids] is not how science works—it's how politics works" (p. A6).

In the United Kingdom, Parliament adopted a national curriculum in 1988 following 8 years of debate. The new history curriculum attempted to strike a balance between memorizing past English monarchs and teaching children how to engage in critical thinking within the discipline of history. This stance drew fire from neoconservatives who demanded that the school's "main mission [was] to transmit to children the country's proud heritage and to reaffirm those collective memories that would make young people loyally and confidently *British*" (Nash, Crabtree, & Dunn, 1997, p. 138). The curriculum that finally came to be adopted excluded the "study of ethnic and religious minority communities and their historical experience" (p. 144).

Such episodes point to the issue Bourdieu addressed on many fronts. First, he outlined the lopsided influence of various groups within the larger society in putting their version of culture into the official school curriculum and imposing it on everyone else (Bourdieu & Passeron, 1970/2000). Second, he underscored how forms of cultural capital were expressions of power and were interconnected with economic capital (Bourdieu, 1986).

Schools graduate students and give them diplomas for the acquisition of the "right" knowledge and proper attitude toward themselves and others. Schools are battlegrounds where social classes will be able to impose their view of the world and their group's place in it, because schools legitimize that view as they inculcate students with the approved and sanctified knowledge of the world. So the question isn't, "Will history be taught?" but, rather, "Whose history will be taught?"

Bourdieu's sociological assertion was that educational instruction and qualifications, together with the institutions attended, help reinforce prevailing social structures and positions, a situation illustrated in both the United States and United Kingdom throughout their recent histories, as we shall see. This view is not unique to Bourdieu and has long been the subject of debate. For instance, Reimer (1971) argued that "schools define merit in accordance with the structure of the society served by schools," adding that "merit is a smoke screen for the perpetuation of privilege" (p. 43) Those social groupings occupying more elevated positions predicated by forms of capital have the ability to ensure that the established "value" structure of academic routes and qualifications is reproduced, thereby retaining their own position of dominance. Merit is bullshit

THE BATTLE OVER THE CORRECT ACADEMIC SUBJECTS AND PROPER PEDAGOGIC WORK

Not only is the nature of specific topics in the school contested, because they are connected to the value-based positions of the world vision of a specific social class, but also what constitutes the "correct" or "proper" cluster of subjects. These groupings are often connected to the perceived nature of pedagogic work, as we shall see in the following examples.

In 2013, the new British coalition government headed by the Conservative Party introduced plans to alter the nature of what it termed "traditional academic" subjects. For example, the party argued that the teaching of English should include a more rigorous focus on spelling, punctuation, and grammar. The education secretary at the time, Michael Gove, expressed strong objections to what he termed the "infantilisation" of the school curriculum, illustrated by such concerns as too few schoolchildren studying pre–20th century novels.

Indeed, in his changes to the history curriculum, Gove is charged with ignoring all guidance and constructing the content himself to include a strong emphasis on memorizing names, dates, and facts. Gove suggested that curriculum reforms should be couched in terms of a return to an age of high educational standards and rigor, creating a "gold standard" qualification that referred to a curriculum and qualification frame originally devised in the 1950s, a harking back to a mythical "golden age" of education familiar in political rhetoric today. *Nostalgia* .

Similar concerns were echoed in the U.S. debate regarding the Common Core curriculum standards. In one high-ranking state, Massachusetts, the English standards would "reduce by 60% the amount of classic literature, poetry, and drama that students will read. For example, the Common Core ignores the novels of Charles Dickens, Edith Wharton, and Mark Twain's *Huckleberry Finn*." It is feared that this proposed curriculum will impair student test achievement in Massachusetts, where "students became the first to score best in the nation in all grades and categories on the National Assessment of Educational Progress" (Gass & Chieppo, 2013, p. A15).

Educational systems in all nations function as constellations of individuals, groups, and agencies vying for position and influence. It is a field of struggle, and the relative positions of influence are anchored in forms of power, the chief of which is economic materialism—that is, wealth based on money and the influence money can buy. But economic materialism is only one form of power.

Bourdieu's work included the idea of cultural capital; for example, noneconomic or nonmaterial aspects of power and education are one form of cultural capital, which is both a means and ends of power. That old saying, "Knowledge is power," typifies this notion. Becoming educated is therefore the acquisition of a form of nonmaterial power. But at some point education is also translated into economic capital, because educational certificates and degrees tend to confer greater influence and material wealth over time.

So education is itself an expression of power. It is not a culturally neutral social space open equally to all who seek to enter; rather, it is a structured set of experiences framed and sanctioned within an institutional and bureaucratic social space. Bourdieu was one of the first to notice the presence of forms of *linguistic capital*—that is, the acquisition of language in the home and its connection to acquisition of language in schools, and the importance of this connection. If the language used in the home mirrors that used in school, then "it follows logically that the educational mortality rate can only increase as one moves towards the classes most distant from scholarly language" (Bourdieu & Passeron, 1970/2000, p. 73). In later chapters in this book, we will explore the various forms of capital at work in education and how they influence what schools do and how various agencies and individuals think schools can be changed or reformed.

THE CONCEPT OF MISRECOGNITION AND HOW IT WORKS

The mechanism of social reproduction is further facilitated by Bourdieu's concept of **misrecognition**, which explains how the fundamental structure of socioeconomic inequality, defined and working within distinctive social/professional fields, is reproduced in the schools. Misrecognition has been defined as

> the form of forgetting that social agents are caught up in and produced by. When we feel comfortable within our roles within the social world they seem to us like second nature and we forget how we have actually been produced as particular kinds of people. (Webb et al., p. xiv)

Despite the usual egalitarian rhetoric about schools being the ladder to the good life for all children of all people, they have rarely, if ever, actually worked that way. Bourdieu was not the first to gather empirical data about how schooling benefited some social groups more than others.

For example, in 1968, Michael Katz published his research on an 1860 town meeting in Beverly, Massachusetts, where the eligible voters approved a motion to abolish the town's 2-year-old, tax-supported public high school. Through an examination of town records, Katz was able to show that the 143 citizens who voted against abolishing the high school were largely from the business class and were wealthy in the community. Those who voted in favor of the motion to abolish the high school were mostly working-class people, what we would call today the town's "blue-collar" segment.

Katz (1968) then took this historic vote and contrasted it with the prevailing reform rhetoric of those times, which was filled with claims regarding what a publicly supported high school would do to bring about greater equal opportunity for all groups of students in Massachusetts. He showed that working-class voters clearly saw it had benefited only a few students, most of them from the wealthy part of Beverly. Katz subsequently commented:

> Surely, high school promoters could not really have expected that the children of factory operatives and laborers would attend. They knew only too well the apathy of these people toward education. In this situation their ideology served partly as a rationalization. By stressing that high schools were democratic, that they fostered equality of

opportunity, educational promoters could cover personal motives with the noblest of sentiments. What they were doing was spreading throughout the whole community the burden of educating a small minority of its children. (p. 53)

The advancement of one agenda without fully understanding who actually benefits from it, and without recognizing that the advocates are the ones who benefit most, is an example of the Bourdieusian concept of misrecognition.

SOME HISTORY WITH MISRECOGNITION

High school advocates in Beverly, Massachusetts, advanced the argument for tax-supported high school on the grounds that it would benefit all children, when in reality it would benefit only a few—their own. Opponents, at least in Beverly, saw quite clearly that their children were not likely to benefit. More than a hundred years later, Christopher Jencks and his colleagues (1972) published a widely read book on inequality in which they stated, "Schools serve primarily as selection and certification agencies whose job is to measure and label people, and only secondarily as socialization agencies whose job is to change people. This implies that schools serve primarily to legitimize inequality, not to create it" (p. 135). To this day, not much has changed about how schools serve to reflect, reinforce, and advance existing socioeconomic inequalities (Greer, 1972; Harris, 1982; Lareau, 2011; Lucas, 1999). The long history of the schooling process illustrates that schools are the means—the tools, if you will—by which those with political power and control legitimize the continuation of their own privilege by controlling the content and process of schooling. While some may perceive the language game being played with "leave no child behind," in reality the same children as before will be left behind (Smith, 2013). The idea that schools were once successful and now are "failing" is a myth. This myth has been used to advance the neoliberal ideas of standardized testing and pay-for-performance plans as an antidote to school failure (Kumashiro, 2008; Prier, 2012; Rotberg, 2011). But as Herbert J. Gans (1972) clearly illustrated in his foreword to *The Great School Legend* (Greer, 1972), released more than 30 years ago, "the public schools of the late nineteenth and early twentieth centuries did not help poor children, but instead, failed them in large numbers and forced them out of the school" (p. vii).

Greer (1972) examined the data and noted that

> the successful selection of losers in this society has been as much an indicator of the school's success as the selection of winners. Excessive real mobility is a great danger to the status quo—and the public schools in America cannot be characterized by their willingness to threaten the propriety of things as they are. (p. 106)

Grant's (1988) school biography of Hamilton High, established in 1953 in a middle-class suburban district near Pittsburgh, Pennsylvania, similarly revealed the presence of the social class structure. Grant's portrait mirrored Coleman's (1961) research on school and the teenage subculture, about which he wrote that in a middle-class school a "boy or girl in such a system finds it governed by an elite whose backgrounds exemplify, in the extreme, those of the dominant population group" (p. 217). Grant (1988) observed that in the 1950s Hamilton High was a place where

> fewer than 15 percent of its students would have been classified as working class. . . . These students either dropped out of school when at age sixteen they were permitted to do so, or they attempted to emulate the leaders in a bid for social mobility. (p. 15)

The impact of social classes using schools to legitimate their position is not confined to Anglo-American or European schools. Rohlen's (1983) study of Japanese high schools similarly illustrated how "the children of the wealthy are doing well, by and large, in education" (p. 139). Rohlen noted:

> The social gap between Kobe's high- and low-status high schools is indeed great—a separation as large as between nineteenth-century classes, European or Japanese. The gap is certainly not just academic. Past and future status, income, and power are involved, and between the elite schools and the vocational schools there is a significant difference in self-esteem and personal conduct. . . . The magnitude of the subcultural differences between types of high schools makes them the modern equivalent of nineteenth-century industrial classes. (pp. 139–140)

Another example is found in India. In 2009, India passed the Right to Education Act, which established that 35% of school admissions must be set aside for low-income students. So far, the results of this intention to use schooling as a means of confronting the wealth gap are disappointing. Teachers in the schools serving large numbers of children from the wealthy sectors of Indian society complain that even at age 4, the children from poor families are way behind in learning fundamentals and social skills (Anand, 2011).

Parents of the more privileged class complain that the presence of the low-income students holds their children back from learning more at school. The differences in cultural capital were evident when teachers at one school asked their class of young children to name things that were colored purple:

> The rich kids shouted out "blackberries," "blackcurrant ice cream" and "potassium permanganate," a chemical used to clean fruits and vegetables. None of the seven low-income kids raised their hands. Unlike the wealthier children, they hadn't learned their colors at home, spoke no English, and were further confused by examples of things they had never heard of. (p. A10)

That schools reinforce existing social classes or groups is largely an accepted notion among most serious scholars examining test score differences internationally (Condron, 2011; Sahlberg, 2011). The conventionally held view of the relationship between schools and social class can be summarized in the influential work by Bowles and Gintis (1976), who commented that schools fostered inequality that was legitimated by an apparent meritocratic approach to rewarding and promoting students and then assigning them distinct positions in the extant social hierarchy. In performing this function, they created and reinforced the existing social class divisions and perpetuated "patterns of social class, racial and sexual identification among students which allow them to relate 'properly' to their eventual standing in the hierarchy of authority and status in the production process" (p. 11).

Bourdieu's notions of class differed from the typical Marxian view advanced by Bowles and Gintis. He also suggested that Marxism posited a raw and crude form of economic determinism and domination, proffering that

> the submission of workers, women, minorities, and graduate students is most often not a deliberate or conscious concession to the brute force of managers, men, whites and professors; it resides, rather, in the unconscious fit between their habitus and the field they operate in. It is deep inside the socialized body. (Wacquant, 1992, p. 24)

Thus, Bourdieu (1989b) wrote, "if it is fitting to recall that the dominated always contribute to their own domination, it is necessary at once to be reminded that the dispositions which incline them to this complicity are also the effect, embodied, of domination" (p. 12).

Bourdieu rejected theories that rested on assumptions that social agents within fields of power or between different fields always behave consciously, rationally, and intentionally to obtain specified goals or objectives. He was therefore at odds with rational-choice models of decision making that were centered on economic models solely motivated by material gain. Rather, Bourdieu's relational approach revolved around his ideas of *habitus, capital,* and *field,* concepts we will explore in greater detail in the following chapters.

A relatively recent example is evident in the acerbic exchange between Turkey's Prime Minister Recep Tayyip Erdoğan and German Chancellor Angela Merkel over the utter lack of Turkish secondary schools in Germany, despite the fact that Germany's Turkish population of 2.5 million (3% of the total German population) is the European Union's largest Turkish community. Stevens (2010) reported that "many Germans . . . resent Turks' many segregated neighborhoods and high rates of unemployment, and feel many don't try hard enough to adapt to Germans' way of life, or even learn the German language" (p. A9).

Students of Turkish descent in German schools tend to perform at lower levels of achievement than their German equivalents, and only 13% of Turkish students make it to the top-level secondary schools, called gymnasiums. In addition, the unemployment rate for the Turkish population is estimated to be nearly double that for native Germans. There are no public schools that teach Turkish students in Turkish. In the larger political world, Germany has also opposed Turkey's entrance as a full-fledged partner in the European Union. The antagonism between the Turkish minority and the German majority involves capital, culture, and fields of power, a conflict that spills over into higher levels of politics in Europe.

BUILDING AWARENESS OF THE FORCES AT PLAY

The purpose of describing the forces at play within the Bourdieusian lens is not to find enemies or scapegoats. Bourdieu's sociology is about accurate description and portrayal to create improved understanding and the possibility of real change. Some critics have charged that Bourdieu is "deterministic," in that his descriptions appear to leave little room for change (see Jenkins, 2002, pp. 117–119). We demur in this regard, because real change begins with as realistic an understanding as possible of the social forces one wishes to alter.

Bourdieu (1990b) was fond of quoting French philosopher Martial Gueroult on this score:

> I cannot at all approve of the fact that people try to deceive themselves by feeding on false imaginings. That is why, seeing that it is a greater perfection to know the truth, even when it is to our disadvantage, than not to know it, I confess that it is better to be less happy and to have more knowledge. (p. 188)

Bourdieu himself worked toward a metanoia—that is, a new vision or understanding—because without it, a real transformation is not likely to occur. The first real change happens within the leader's mind. The practitioner has to find "new eyes" for continuing problems and issues. With new eyes comes the development of new solutions (see Bolton, 2011).

WITHOUT NEW EYES: THE BLINDERS OF DOXA AS ORTHODOXY

In Bourdieu's corpus, **doxa** refers to the prevailing orthodoxies at work in any field. All fields have prevailing modes of thought and generally accepted remedies for an array of problems, whether they work or not. Such remedies are often perceived as generically true and necessary for success. "For Bourdieu, the **'doxic attitude'** means bodily and unconscious submission to conditions that are in fact quite arbitrary and contingent" (Webb et al., 2002, p. xi).

In the history of science, some of these mental constructs have been called *paradigms* (Kuhn, 1996). Kuhn showed that while the use of some paradigms helped solve problems, in other cases it blocked problem solving. Paradigms are simply "lenses"—that is, peculiar "glasses" we look through to solve problems. Some glasses prevent us from seeing all the dimensions of a problem because humans don't problem-solve with an open mind. Problem solving begins with all our previous experiences, conditioning, and narratives serving as filters to any kind of work we do. Humans come to problem solving with their minds filled with lived past experiences and "classificatory schemes, systems of classification, the fundamental oppositions of thought, masculine/feminine, right/left, east/west," and so on (Bourdieu, 1990b, p. 25). In short, our minds are crowded with a great deal of cultural and conceptual clutter, and too often we are completely unaware of it. We don't think reflexively; that is, we don't think about *how* we are thinking.

NO Metacognition

Instead, we think about things, actions, or outcomes. Bourdieu tried very hard to subject his own thinking to scrutiny before he thought about anything. This is the difference between reflexivity and reflectivity. True reform and change begin with reflexivity, which is the beginning of having "new eyes."

Doxa are simply the "rules of the game, meaning that specific forms of struggle are legitimized whereas others are excluded" (Swartz, 1997, p. 125). It is instructive to note that in mid-2010, all the "reform" strategies considered by the Barack Obama administration in turning around so-called "failing schools" began with firing the school principal. When queried as to the research base substantiating this position, Obama officials couldn't come up with any (Flanary, 2010). Bourdieu (1971) observed that "what attaches a thinker to his age, what situates and dates him, is above all the kind of problems and themes in terms of which he is obliged to think" (pp. 182–183). Firing the principal is an approach preferred in the world of business, and the Obama administration Department of Education was staffed with many ex-officials from foundations and businesses, or those who had training in business (English, 2014).

BOURDIEU AS THE PUBLIC INTELLECTUAL, ACTIVIST, AND PROVOCATEUR

Bourdieu's academic brilliance and his reputation on issues of social justice in France led him to speak out in the popular media against the emerging forces of neoliberalism and globalization that enjoyed popularity in the United States, United Kingdom, and Australia (Mullen, Samier, Brindley, English, & Carr, 2013). Increasingly, Bourdieu spoke out publicly to renounce the harmful impact of privatization of government services and to advocate for protection of the least able to protect themselves in the public arena (Lane, 2006).

Bourdieu spoke of the "left hand" and the "right hand" of the state in this struggle. He characterized those on the "left hand" as public officials, teachers, and social workers who were pitted against the "right hand" as represented by the politicians, technocrats, bankers, and think-tank pundits. At stake in this struggle was the ethos of "public service," which had been the watchword of the state and was now under direct attack. Bourdieu lumped both Marxists and neoliberals into one hostile camp because both "were forms of economism" and led to the triumph of economic models as the arbiter of social good.

The irony of Bourdieu's life is that, at the end of his career, he engaged in a defense of the French educational system and programs of government that he had built his reputation on critiquing for their failure to live up to their ideals (Lane, 2006, p. 26). He discerned that the influence of neoliberalism was a greater threat to the ideals of France than their reform or abandonment because neoliberalism threatened the total erasure of those ideals. ? *Need clarification*

Bourdieu's life was a self-imposed trial of discovery and a dogmatic pursuit of reality. In this pursuit he was not afraid to confront established dogma, to challenge cherished beliefs, or to pursue lines of thought and inquiry that made sense to him. He was not a perfect man or a perfect academic; yet what makes Bourdieu worth the effort is that even within his pessimism based on observations of how school systems worked to reinforce the social and cultural dominance of certain powerful groups, he found reason to believe change was possible. Thus, his ideas and ideals are worth reading and understanding because, in doing so, the promises for improved public education can be realized. Bourdieu (1990b) summarized this perspective well when he remarked about challenging various classifications, "It is in discovering its historicity that reason gives itself the means of escaping from history" (p. 25).

That change begins with an understanding of how the system works, which is the subject of the next chapter.

IMPLICATIONS FOR POLICY AND PRACTICE

A Social World of Policy and Practice That Is Dynamic, Fluid, and Contested

Bourdieu presents a sociological picture of the world of educational policy and practice as contested and dynamic. Teachers, administrators, parents, politicians, policy wonks, and self-defined neoliberal billionaires work in a volatile social space where forms of capital are expended to influence policy and practice. There will be no end to this contestation because, as Bourdieu points out, there is no supra agency that will bestow final legitimacy on any perspective or group's agenda. To prevail in this contested social space, individuals, groups, and agencies have to expend their resources to influence others to adopt their point of view, or compel them using various forms of power to adopt or accept their agenda.

Repressive and Discriminatory Educational Practices Persist Because Even Those Who Are Disadvantaged by Them Accept Them as "Legitimate"

Those persons or groups not well served by the school and its practices accept them anyway and in so doing legitimize and perpetuate them. That the dominated participate in their own domination is one of Bourdieu's key insights into how schools continue to function even as they underserve the larger society. One example is that Black males are continually suspended and disciplined in schools at rates way out of proportion to their actual numbers, but the routines and beliefs of the school that led to those suspensions and disciplinary procedures are rarely questioned as appropriate, even by Black males. The form of resistance adopted by Black males is considered aberrant and detrimental even by them (see Fergus & Noguera, 2010). Bourdieu (1980/1990a) described this feature when he said, "The dominated are dominated in their brains too" (p. 41). *internalized repression.*

School Practitioners Are Part of the Problem if They Don't See How Schools Really Work

Most school practitioners work in schools because they are part of the ethic of public service. Most believe in the promise of schooling to enhance the lives of young people. Few enter education to get rich. Work in schools represents a kind of special "calling," one firmly anchored in the idea of progress and the advancement of humanity. And few educators would deny the power of education in helping their students advance both economically and socially in their respective societies.

However, it is amazing how many school practitioners who work very hard in schools don't see how their work reinforces the existing class divisions and economic disparities in the larger society. They are blinded by the rhetoric of their own calling. Bourdieu called all those claims into question when he presented the data on who advances and who benefits the most from schooling, by social class. His data, now several decades dated, are mirrored again and again in current data gathered in the United Kingdom and United States. The well-to-do receive the most benefit from state-sponsored school systems. Historical data strongly suggest that this has been the case since the establishment of public education.

For school practitioners to begin moving in different directions and more objectively examine their own behaviors and actions, the connection between schooling and the larger social divisions mu seen in its entirety and with greater clarity than before. Practitioners must see that many of the so-called "reforms" are merely warmed-over calls to reinforce existing behavior and will continue to benefit the children of the privileged. The children of the poor don't need more rigor in schooling; they need more relevance. The development of a different set of eyes regarding the function of schooling is to ask trenchantly, who is proposing changes and who will benefit most from them? Furthermore, whose voice is being heard and whose voice is silent or absent from any discussion of change? Those questions should help reveal the true beneficiaries of educational "reforms" being debated in policy discussions in both the United Kingdom and United States.

KEY CHAPTER CONCEPTS

doxa, the doxic attitude

Doxa are the core beliefs, attitudes, principles, or concepts considered true and proper regarding the nature and relationships of things. The *doxic attitude* encompasses the often unstated but shared beliefs about how practices in schools should be defined, advanced, and/or evaluated. This attitude is usually unquestioned and accepted as a given.

In *Masculine Domination*, Bourdieu (2001) spoke of the *paradox of doxa*, which is that the "order of the world as we find it . . . is broadly respected" (p. 1). He insightfully remarked that

> the established order, with its relations of domination, its rights and prerogatives, privileges and injustices, ultimately perpetuates itself so easily, apart from a few historical accidents, and that the most intolerable conditions of existence can so often be perceived as acceptable and even natural. (p. 1)

In schools, a doxic attitude can be seen when the appalling rates of African American and Latino school failure, suspension, and dropout rates are considered acceptable and the "way it is" by both the dominant members of the culture and the unfortunate recipients of practices that have led to these conditions (the dominated). An excellent review of the doxic attitude as Bourdieu lived it in France appears in Grenfell (2007, pp. 152–171).

misrecognition

On the face of it, Bourdieu's concept of *misrecognition* seems fairly simple; actually, it is anything but simple. Misrecognition refers to the use of symbolic power and language as a symbol of its expression. The social world is one of structures and exists in hierarchies of domination and submission, of vying and competing political and socioeconomic interests that are interacting within a given social space.

Here is Bourdieu's (1991) explanation:

> The institutionalized circle of collective misrecognition, which is the basis of belief in the value of an ideological discourse, is established only when the structure of the field of production and circulation of this discourse is such that the negation it effects (by saying what it says only in a form which suggests that it is not saying it) is brought together with interpreters who are able, as it were, to misrecognize again the negated message; in other words, the circle is established only when what is denied by the form is 're-miscognized', that is, known and recognized in the form, and only in the form, in which it is realized by denying itself. (p. 153)

We can think of several examples of this. When regressive neoliberal policies speak of free markets and liberation but in practice what is meant is that public space is commodified and sold to those who want to make a profit, the true intention is concealed. When others repeat these words and fail to see how their implementation negates what is desired, *that is misrecognition.* The contradiction, the negation of the message contained within the message itself, is not revealed and remains hidden. Bourdieu (1991) summarizes this circumstance by saying, "Ideological production is all the more successful when it is able to *put in the wrong* anyone who attempts to *reduce* it to its objective truth" (p. 153).

In the case of the development of leadership standards in the United Kingdom and United States, the language of the standards seems to be about optimizing the strengths of individual schools, but it is really about making all the schools the same (English, 2003).

2

Unmasking the School Asymmetry and the Social System

❖ ❖ ❖

WHAT THIS CHAPTER IS ABOUT

Schools have not been socially constructed places designed to foment revolution, foster major social change, or rectify issues of inequality or wealth disparities. Rather, despite the political rhetoric of social change used by advocates or reformers professing education as a means to equity and "fairness," schools have continually reinforced the socio-economic status quo (Brantlinger, 2003; Savage & English, 2013).

Practitioners need to look carefully at how schools really work and untangle beliefs and procedures that are often contradictory. For example, if tests are culturally biased, their continued use in grouping students will perpetuate discrimination against children of the poor. If test results are then used to determine teacher pay based on test performance, the impact is compounded, as teachers of poor children will continue to receive less pay for their work. And the poor will become poorer because there are disincentives to teach them.

The attitudes students experience in the home, the adoption of unspoken dispositions about the value of education or the need to obtain a quality education to advance in the larger society, are major determinants of school success. Likewise, teacher attitudes and values toward children of poverty and those with limited privilege in schools work to reinforce the achievement disparity based on students' socioeconomic positions. These predispositions are not easily overcome and may be reinforced with such legislation as No Child Left Behind or Race to the Top, or implementation of the Common Core curriculum standards.

This chapter indicates how Pierre Bourdieu's pioneering work with schools and the larger social structure is interconnected. Through the sociological lens Bourdieu created, we will examine common issues facing formal educational systems in many countries. We will use this lens as a framework to examine specific educational concerns and explore promising paths for discussing how they might be resolved.

Specifically, this chapter addresses the following points:

- Children of the dominant elite find the culture of school to be familiar and accessible, while children from nondominant groups may find it alienating and contentious.

- Schools serve as a legitimizing agency for the imposition of a cultural arbitrary representative of the politically dominant interest groups that rationalize their own control and misrecognize this imposition as being best for everyone.

- Those who are not successful in schools are accused of being incapable and unable to carry out the tasks of school compliance because of a variety of personal deficits (real or imagined), including possessing the wrong attitude or lacking intelligence.

- Any reform or proposed change in the fundamental mission of the school that threatens the interests or social position of the dominant groups will be co-opted or opposed, sometimes labeled with the political rhetoric of "antidemocratic" or "antimeritocratic." Any proposal to spread out social advantage more broadly will be resisted and opposed.

INTRODUCTION

Educators working within schools often see them wrapped in the rhetoric of "what should be" instead of "what is." This tendency is reinforced by the prevailing ideology of school leadership in which school principals or headmasters are urged to engage in "visioning" exercises as part of demonstrating leadership (Shipman, Queen, & Peel, 2007, p. 17). This practice, however, is about envisioning what the school or schools "ought to be" instead of taking a clear and hard-headed look at what they actually do. In this environment it is easy for school leaders to misunderstand or misrecognize the nature of the challenges facing them.

The battle for what schools do, what curricula they employ, and how they treat different groups of children is a reflection of a larger ongoing sociopolitical contestation that must be viewed in the time and context of any review. Schools therefore represent places of conflict and friction culturally, socially, economically, and politically. In short, schools are not neutral agencies functioning in neutral social spaces. More than 30 years ago, Reimer (1971) remarked of this phenomenon,

> School necessarily sorts its students into a caste-like hierarchy of privilege. There may be nothing wrong with hierarchy or with privilege, or even with hierarchies of privilege, so long as these are plural and relatively independent of each other. There is everything wrong with a dominant hierarchy of privilege to which all others must conform. (p. 42)

What Bourdieu's research revealed was the façade of neutrality that cloaks how schools work to perpetuate the socioeconomic status quo, and how they continue to do so even as contemporary political rhetoric fosters the idea of family choice, vouchers, and other such market-based mechanisms as an antidote to the legitimacy of social inequality (Barry, 2005; Prier, 2012; Ravitch, 2010b, 2012).

Bourdieu brought a more discerning gaze to what schools do. He pursued a research agenda that revealed the asymmetrical relationship between the schools and the social groups within the larger social system. By this he meant that networks of influence and power are not equally distributed among all groups of people but instead exist disproportionately. Some groups or social classes are better placed to shape the schools so they reflect their own ideas of what is important, thereby reinforcing and preserving their social position in the larger society through the schools. Bourdieu's work helps us question how this situation arises and, indeed, how it persists despite the honest efforts of some to change it.

BOURDIEUSIAN CORNERSTONES

Bourdieu considered education to be of central importance as a mechanism for transmitting and reproducing the values, dispositions, and relations of social spaces from one generation to the next. To explain how these mechanisms work, Bourdieu devised three key concepts: habitus, field, and capital. He explained that while his philosophy was "condensed" into these concepts, "its cornerstone is the two-way relationship between objective structures (those of social fields) and incorporated structures (those of the habitus)" (Bourdieu, 1998b, p. vii). Together, the concepts create a "logic of practice" and while each of the concepts will be explained here separately, this should not be interpreted to mean they are stand-alone ideas; they are not.

Bourdieu's methodology is interrelational and interdependent, because the interplay among his key trio of concepts is necessary for understanding the social world. Thus, it is inevitable that as you read through this book, these concepts will keep on reappearing as we use them to examine different aspects of education systems and practices. We will begin in this chapter by explaining two of the key elements of this trio: habitus and field. Capital will be discussed in Chapter 4.

BOURDIEU'S CONCEPT OF HABITUS

How a person's life expectations and chances are shaped within any given culture is contained in that individual's life space or **habitus**, a provocative Bourdieusian construct postulating that a person's dispositions— tendencies to act or respond in certain ways under certain conditions or circumstances—were established without that person necessarily being conscious of them or being directed to adhere to them.

In Bourdieu's (1980/1990a) terms, "they can be collectively orchestrated without being the product of the organizing action of a conductor" (p. 53), and the question of how this was possible, how society functions without overt intervention, was of core interest to Bourdieu. His concept of habitus stems from this central question. It comprises both a "structured and structuring structure," by which he meant that habitus is "structured" by our past and upbringing but also "structuring," as it helps shape our future (Bourdieu, 1984, p. 170).

Bourdieu deliberately selected the term *structure* to emphasize that habitus is not random but has patterns and is in many ways predictable in generating perceptions and attitudes, or, as Bourdieu termed them, dispositions. These dispositions are both lasting, or "durable," and "transposable" to other fields and social spheres. Habitus is transmitted "without passing through language or consciousness" but, rather, is "inscribed in our bodies, in things, in situations and everyday lives" (Bourdieu, 1991, p. 51).

AN EXAMPLE OF NEIGHBORHOOD HABITUS

An illustration of the influence of Bourdieu's habitus is apparent in Wilson's (1987, 1996) theory of neighborhood effects. Wilson postulated that as middle-class White families abandoned inner-city neighborhoods, these neighborhoods became havens for racially segregated, disadvantaged populations that were largely if not exclusively African American, female-headed families with children—often characterized by acute poverty and joblessness—leading to a sense of alienation for this group.

Wilson's theory indicated that because there were few, if any, role models for African American adolescents in these inner-city neighborhoods, they did not understand the benefits of schooling and social advancement. "These views thereby breed sentiments of fatalism and hopelessness about the benefits of education and what can be accomplished with additional schooling" (Stewart, Stewart, & Simons, 2007, p. 900).

A study of Wilson's theory, involving 39 neighborhood clusters in two states, showed that neighborhood structural conditions were significantly related to educational aspirations and that these conditions functioned apart from any effects of individual characteristics. Specifically, the more disadvantaged the neighborhood was, the more negatively impacted educational aspirations were.

Bourdieu's notion of habitus is captured in this empirical study. The neighborhood conditions create a "structuring structure," which creates a predisposition toward schooling, specifically affecting college-level aspirations for youth living there. Clearly, there were no "master orchestrators" requiring adolescents to heed or obey them. The attitudes they acquired were durable and transposable. They saw little benefit in education and so had a reduced desire to pursue it beyond compulsory schooling.

Bourdieu's concept of habitus incorporated the idea of the creation of an internal disposition prompted by external conditions in such a way that these conditions became sustaining or durable and accepted as the way the world works. The logic involved in this often unconscious transfer of values from an external situation to an internal disposition happens in a "durable, systematic and non-mechanical way" (Bourdieu, 1980/1990a, p. 55).

Thus, the habitus is a dynamic, fluid, powerful concept that explains how the cycle of poverty and negative attitudes toward schooling are perpetuated without the presence of a master organizer.

A CASE STUDY OF HOW FAMILY HABITUS WORKS TO SHAPE CAREER ASPIRATIONS

A recent study in the United Kingdom showed how family habitus affects aspirations for a career in science (Archer et al., 2012). "Family habitus" in this study was defined as an exploratory notion of how "families construct a collective relationship with science and the extent to which this is shaped by their possession of particular sorts of economic, social, and cultural capital" (p. 886). The study employed both quantitative and qualitative data sources. The quantitative data were based on a survey of 9,000 parents and students. These data revealed that slightly more than half the variance (50.5%) reported that the most important variables for positive student aspirations in science were parental attitudes toward science, experiences of school science, and student self-concept in science.

A second part of this U.K. study was qualitative and based on 160 semistructured interviews with 78 parents and 92 children age 10 or Year 6 in the U.K. school system. The data from these semistructured interviews indicated that

> middle-class families' economic, social, and cultural capital enabled children to participate in a greater volume and variety of science-related extracurricular activities. . . . The interplay of family habitus and (often substantial) science-specific cultural and social capital produced a sense of science being "what we do" and "who we are." (Archer et al., 2012, p. 891)

community capital

The study further noted that "in such families, the alignment between family habitus, capital, and the child's personal interests and identification produces a strong, mutually reinforcing consensus, which is also embodied and realized through emotional bonds and practices" (Archer et al., 2012, p. 892).

Conversely, the same study noted, "in our sample the majority of children who did not express science aspirations came from working-class backgrounds" (Archer et al., 2012, p. 900). To quote the study more fully,

> We suggest that the limits of possibility [to identify with science and a potential career in science] are even more constrained for working-class families where the interplay of family habitus and the unequal distribution of both generic and science-specific capital in society means that for a sizeable proportion of working-class families and children, science is simply an "unthinkable" aspiration. (p. 899)

An important conclusion from this study was that the researchers did not find that family habitus was deterministic—that is, that it was always the case that children from working-class families or middle-class families showed no variance in their aspirations toward science as a result of their social class position. There were exceptions, but as the researchers observed, "the interplay of family capital and habitus—while by no means deterministic—does provide a powerful structuring context that influences how children formulate their aspirations" (Archer et al., 2012, p. 904).

This finding resonates with Bourdieu's own belief that while social agents live under the constraints of habitus and field dynamics, habitus is not static. Indeed, he stated that "habitus is not a destiny" (Bourdieu, 2000, p. 180); rather, it is evolutionary, constantly changing. So while it determines practice and position, it is also determined by it:

> There is an ongoing adaptation process as habitus encounters new situations, but this process tends to be slow, unconscious, and tends to elaborate rather than alter fundamentally the primary dispositions. (Swartz, 1997, p. 107)

Thus, while social agents play the hand dealt them, they might also take advantage of opportunities, as Bourdieu himself did when he escaped his own habitus to gain substantial symbolic capital and status within the academic field.

THE INTERSECTION OF CLASS AND SOCIAL SPACE/FIELD

While we will refer to class as Bourdieu did, it is important to note he argued that his notion of class differed from the perhaps more familiar Marxian concept. Thus, an earlier popular definition of class offered by Bowles and Gintis (1976)—"a group of individuals who relate to the production process in similar ways. A class structure emerges naturally from the institutions of U.S. capitalism" (p. 67)—would be rejected by Bourdieu as a form of economism (i.e., simple economic determinism).

Bourdieu's concept of habitus helps further illustrate his notions of class, which, as previously explained, differ from the Marxian approach. He argued that habitus can be a "collective habitus," where similarities in history and mutual experience form a similar habitus for some groups with shared interests and values, but that this does not constitute a social class "in the sense of being a group, a group mobilised for struggle" (Bourdieu, 1991, p. 229); rather, these groups simply share common experiences and beliefs. Such shared experiences mean that groups will tend to behave collectively or respond to situations similarly, but this does not necessarily mean they are organized, acting consciously, or "mobilised for struggle."

Bourdieu (1998b) further rejected this definition and the Marxian line of argument as "a false theoretical solution" (p. 11) required by Marx to take action on a real or perceived problem of any particular social group. To construct an action agenda with group solidarity, Marx presented the group (i.e., the proletariat) as a historical force supported by the construction of the concept of class itself.

Instead of the traditional notion of class, Bourdieu substituted the concept of social space. This shift enabled him to discuss social differentiation, which was not the same in every society in the world, and to present the varying groups that vied with one another as dynamic and contested within a field (Bourdieu, 1998). He argued that there was a grave danger of classifying social groups by various features, in particular economic ones, as he considered that such classes could be only "theoretical" and did not exist in the real world.

This notion of a theoretical class reflects his assertion that classifying a class on the basis of income, for example, did not make everybody within this classification the same and that treating them as if they were would obfuscate difference. Instead, he argued for the idea of "a social space, a space of difference" in which social agents could navigate between social structures and power relations (Bourdieu, 1998b, p. 11).

This idea of social space or **field** is a key concept in Bourdieu's sociology. Fields are networks or configurations that impose values and rules in specific social spaces. These values and rules are at the center of how power and influence are defined among the agents in that field (Bourdieu & Wacquant, 1992). The role of the field concept in Bourdieu's sociological lexicon was to show the ways social relationships are largely representative of conflict, as "fields of struggle" where agents or players in Bourdieu's social space compete.

A field has its own logic and its own agents or players. The competition centers on influence, and the participants work to establish and extend their influence and power within the field (Wacquant, 1992, p. 17). A field, therefore, is a "space of play" and not just empty space; it is fluid and also governed by the interaction of habitus and the structure of the social space. The structure is established by the interaction of the agents or players in that space, which gives each field a peculiarity of its own.

AN EXAMPLE OF A FIELD WITH ITS OWN LOGIC

One example of a field explored by Bourdieu was the literary field. This is a social space of writers and artists. He approached his research using a three-step procedure: (1) Analyze the positions of the literary field and its derivation over a time period, (2) examine the internal structure of the field, and (3) observe the development of the habitus for agents in various positions within the field (Bourdieu, 1992).

By the internal structure of the field, Bourdieu meant the specific universe that obeyed its own laws of functioning and transformation. This internal structure consisted of the "objective relations between positions occupied by individuals and groups placed in a situation of competition for legitimacy" (Bourdieu, 1992, p. 214).

In studying the development of the habitus for persons within that field, Bourdieu went about researching how the various systems of dispositions worked to create a social trajectory that then translated into a specific position in the field. While Bourdieu (2000) argued that "habitus was not a destiny" (p. 180), he emphasized that any change would be gradual, unconscious, and would only rarely bring about a fundamental shift in a person's dispositions.

In a study of college teachers in the United Kingdom (Bolton, 2013), the resilience of habitus in continuing to influence individuals was evident, as the teachers in the study expressed enduring approaches to education and education systems originating from their own parental influence and early educational experiences. While all the participants in the study were teachers, the differences in their educational experiences and qualifications, together with the subjects they taught and whether those subjects were academic or vocational, demonstrated the continuing impact of habitus.

Those teachers who had progressed from school to university and then went into teaching academic subjects demonstrated confidence in their abilities as teachers and articulated the importance of having the "right" education. Those teachers who had received less direct parental support as children or had taken a more indirect route into teaching via a vocational occupation and lacked formal qualifications were more hesitant in expressing confidence in their teaching and academic capabilities. Indeed, while all these participants were qualified teachers and employed in similar roles, they did perceive differences in the types of qualifications they possessed and taught, and this impacted the "value" they placed on qualifications and their perceptions of the students who acquired vocational or academic qualifications.

The combined impact of habitus and qualification value was similarly reflected in career progressions and, indeed, entry into the teaching field, as possession of a university degree coupled with habitus permitted greater promotion opportunities than were available to those without such valued qualifications. The enhanced capital afforded access to broader, cross-college roles for these teachers and, therefore, access to positions of influence where the almost unconscious value messages relating to qualifications and subject areas were reinforced and perpetuated.

This situation is representative of misrecognition, as these teachers were not deliberately promoting one group of practitioners over another but misrecognized their own position of influence and reinforced their own interests. In this study, while all teachers had opportunities for movement within the field, the teachers with higher qualifications and stronger expression of scholastic habitus were the ones who gained promotion more quickly and achieved the most movement, both within and between fields (Bolton, 2013).

In common with his other major concepts, Bourdieu's notion of field serves as an example of the "blurred" definitions of his ideas and illustrates the evolving nature of his thinking. However, Bourdieu's assertion that "there are as many fields as there are interests" (Bourdieu & Wacquant, 1992, p. 117) makes the concept of field a useful mechanism for "thinking" about different social groupings and learners, and identifying the differing structures and players within these groups. It should be apparent that a field is not a dead space of some sort or an empty one; rather, in Bourdieu's projection, it is a space of play, a location of action and contestation and, ultimately, friction. Bourdieu stressed that "to think in terms of field is to *think relationally*" (Bourdieu & Wacquant, 1992, p. 26). For example, habitus impacts the way people operate within a particular field and their expectations and understanding of the "rules of the game" within the field. Because of this interplay, while Bourdieu did develop ideas relating to social class, he believed that the effects of class background on individual action "are always *mediated* through the structure of fields" (Swartz, 1997, p. 119).

Bourdieu argued that the concept of field affords a more dynamic analysis of societies than more "static" analyses of major institutions or predetermined classifications might offer. The issues relating to "classification" of social groups and how it can lead to false assumptions and "solutions" will be further examined in Chapter 4.

THE CULTURAL ARBITRARY

Cultures are neither neutral nor universal, though they may appear as such to those born into them. This observation was underscored by Edward Hall (1966), who remarked, "Culture hides much more than it reveals, and strangely enough what it hides, it hides most effectively from its own participants" (p. 39).

Human perception does not work outside of culture; rather, culture conditions and shapes perception. This is so because "seeing comes before words. The child looks and recognizes before it can speak"; therefore, nothing is seen "as it is" but only as culture enables it to be perceived (Berger, 1972, p. 7).

Therefore, reality is culturally arbitrary and inwardly defined before it is externally perceived. "Reality" is thus multiperspectival. This fact is at the root of Bourdieu's use of the term **cultural arbitrary** to describe the official state adoption of any particular cultural form as an exercise of symbolic power expressed as a type of political domination—that is, "the pedagogy of authority" asserted through the state.

By incorporating a particular cultural form in the school, it is transformed into a perceived "neutral gaze" and also legitimated as the "official" view of reality. The school is sanctioned as the secular source for final determination of what is and is not the "right" or "correct" interpretation of events, actions, ideas, manners, and dispositions. History taught in schools is the history not to be questioned.

The adoption of a specific cultural frame in a school is a form of value adjudication, a determination beyond any serious questioning, a kind of *metanarrative* that refers to a story or discourse that has become "privileged," in which schools "function to outline what is or is not acceptable, desirable, efficient, and so forth regarding educational discourses-practices" (Cherryholmes, 1988, p. 11).

Schooling—what is taught and how it is taught formally and informally—has been the source of a great deal of cultural conflict. The current debates regarding the Common Core curriculum standards in the United States underscore the nature and intensity of some of that contestation. Bourdieu (1984/2009) also wrote about the "aristocracy of culture" that focuses on noncurriculum, general cultural matters (p. 23). This would include what constitutes "proper" manners: the way children address adults and one another in certain social situations; different expectations based on gender roles, such as what girls can say to one another and to boys, and vice versa; what constitutes "good taste" in forms of communication and artistic representation;

how to respect (or not) manifestations of time; how to appear to work hard and be studious; how to conform (or not) to any teacher's expectations; and what defines appropriate dress and for what occasions.

THE PLIGHT OF MINORITY CHILDREN FACING THE DOMINANT CULTURAL ARBITRARY IN SCHOOLS

The tragic position of some minority students is that as they confront the culture of the school and discern that it is antithetical to that within their family and social class, they are faced with either adopting a cultural value system and outlook that alienates them from their peers and/or families or resisting the school's culture, becoming increasingly disconnected from it and eventually dropping out, thus negating whatever the school might offer them for advancement in the larger social/cultural milieu (Bourdieu & Passeron, 1979; Boykin, 1986; MacLeod, 1987; Prier, 2012; Solomon, 1992).

In New York City, educators learned the hard way that their attempts to teach Chinese children how to share their opinions with adults failed when Chinese parents strongly objected, indicating that children were not allowed to talk at mealtimes and/or to argue with their parents because it was a sign of disrespect (Meyers & Rust, 2000, p. 37).

In England, the cultural clash with students from Gypsy, Roma, or Irish Traveler groups presents a real example of the imposition of Bourdieu's cultural arbitrary in action. These students are the lowest-achieving group in English schools. "They are more likely than any other demographic group to be identified as having special educational needs and are more likely to be excluded from school" (Maddern, 2012, p. 28). The academic records of these very culturally different children show that only 17% of Irish Travelers and 11% of Gypsy and Roma students reach the same level of accomplishment as the national average of 58%.

One official of the Equality and Human Rights Commission said that "discrimination against these communities [Gypsy, Roma, and/or Irish Traveler] appears to be the last respectable form of racism" (Maddern, 2012, p. 30). Brian Foster, chair of the Advisory Council for the Education of Romany and Other Travellers, says that students from these groups are left with the option of "fight, flight or playing white," where the first term means a refusal to adopt the dominant cultural norms of the other, White students (p. 30).

An ethnographic study of literacy rates in Gypsy communities in England clearly demonstrated the nature of Bourdieu's cultural arbitrary. Observations of Gypsy children in schools indicated that they had very different patterns of interaction with adults and "tended to move between classrooms during lessons without permission" (Levinson, 2007, p. 17). Patterns of play among Gypsy children were also distinctive, leading to the claim that "Gypsy children do not know how to play" (p. 17). Gypsy children complained about being isolated from friends, and the school practice of age grading and grouping by ability contrasted with how they lived in their home environments, where there is a high degree of interaction and collaboration. Gypsy children consider the requirement to work alone or in silence to be the most negative aspect of school.

The high school leaving rate for Gypsy, Roma, and Irish Traveler children and their very low achievement rates are echoed in the United States by Hispanic and African American student dropout rates and achievement gaps between those groups and White students (Banchero, 2011; Hechinger, 2007; Sparks, 2011). This kind of disparity can also be seen in other countries, such as Germany, where an article in *The Economist* noted that "a bigger concern [in Germany] is that early selection fails children from poor and immigrant families, who are likeliest to attend the least academic schools and to miss out on apprenticeships" ("Tinker, Tailor, Glass-Eye-Maker," 2011, p. 84). In Hungary, a large number of Roma children "are frequently classified as mentally handicapped, even if they are not. About half of Roma children are segregated and receive a substandard education" ("Hungary's Roma," 2013, p. 47).

This trend has been accentuated in the United States by the resegregation of schools prompted by a U.S. Supreme Court decision in 1991 (*Board of Education of Oklahoma City v. Dowell*) that enabled school systems to negate earlier federal court desegregation mandates (Shannon, 2012). As a result, compared with the early 1990s when Black and Latino students attended schools where about one third of the students were low income, low-income students now account for two thirds of the population in those schools.

Additionally, the rapidly growing Latino population has seen increasing segregation of students recently, particularly in the West. Latino enrollment in public schools has gone up from one-twentieth of U.S. students in 1970 to one-fourth in 2009. In the West, the share of Latino students in such settings has increased almost fourfold . . . from 12 percent in 1968 to 43 percent in 2009. (p. 5)

And these culturally different children are disciplined and expelled from schools at disproportionally high rates (Fergus & Noguera, 2010).

In 1988, Medina commented that the rapid increase in numbers of Hispanic students was accompanied with practices of segregation, high failure rates, and school dropouts that amounted to "Hispanic economic and social apartheid" (p. 346). Recent statistical data indicate that in many American cities, the dropout rates for African American and Latino males are well above 50% (Schott Foundation, 2010).

A recent national study based on the U.S. Department of Education Office for Civil Rights showed that during the 2009–2010 school year African American students were suspended three times more frequently than White students, and there is "evidence that African-American students are punished more severely than other students for minor offenses" (Shah & Maxwell, 2012, p. 6). The same data also indicate that for African American students with disabilities the suspension rate was even higher. "One in four such students was suspended at least once that year" (p. 6).

John Jackson, president of the Schott Foundation for Public Education in Cambridge, Massachusetts, commented on the suspension rates by saying,

> These numbers show clear and consistent racial and ethnic disparities in suspensions across the country. We are not providing [these students] a fair and substantive opportunity to learn. Any entity not serious about addressing this becomes a co-conspirator in the demise of these children. (Shah & Maxwell, 2012, p. 6)

According to an urban school superintendent in the United States, "on every indicator of progress, black males are underrepresented and on every indicator that suggests a problem, black males are overrepresented" (Maxwell, 2012, p. 9). Winfield (2012) summarized this national predicament:

> These are the "unfit" of the modern era and are consistently characterized as lazy, parasitic, promiscuous, uneducable, and in need of surveillance and control. In what can only be described as a direct expression of eugenic ideology, these human beings are regarded not as a mere nuisance; rather, they represent a grave threat to the well-being of the "more deserving" among us. (p. 144)

This perceived threat is femoved by suspension and expulsion. For example, in England "a total of 17 per cent of Irish Travellers and 15 percent of Gypsy or Roma children were suspended from school in the same year . . . compared to 4 per cent of all pupils" (Maddern, 2012, p. 30).

Bourdieu and Passeron (1979) commented on the same phenomenon nearly 50 years earlier:

> Economic obstacles are not sufficient to explain how "education death rates" can differ so widely between one social class and another. Even if there were no other evidence and if we knew nothing of the numerous and often very indirect ways in which the school system steadily eliminates children originating from the least privileged backgrounds, proof of the magnitude of the cultural obstacles which these children have to overcome could be found in the fact that even at the level of higher education, one still finds differences in attitude and ability that are significantly related to social origin, although the students whom they differentiate have all undergone fifteen or twenty years of the standardizing influence of schooling. (p. 8)

In one of Bourdieu's earliest researches on the impact of class and educational attainment, he discerned that social class was a determining factor in how far students from each class were able to go in school. It does not appear surprising to us now, but Bourdieu's data based on advancement in the French university system were eye-opening at the time because they showed that students from the lowest social class were the least successful and the least represented in total numbers in the system.

Thirty-four years later, Smith (2012) observed in the United States that, "at the college level, one-half of the children from high-income families completed college in 2007 versus only 9 percent of low-income families . . . a wider gap than existed in 1989" (p. 71). Maynor (2011) demonstrated the same phenomenon at work in tracking Native American student achievement in North Carolina's public school system.

HOW THE SYSTEM WORKS AS A GAME

Bourdieu argued that the educational system is a type of "game" and we must understand the rules of play to more accurately perceive why such systems engage in the actions they select and exhibit resistance to changing those actions. In short, there is nothing "neutral" or "natural" about how educational systems work. They represent the interests of the groups of people who have the means to define and shape how to sort and select who will succeed and who will not. That they remain obdurate to change efforts also means that those people working within the schools or supporting what they do like what they do.

Despite the rhetoric of many of the educational reformers of many nations who espouse egalitarian proposals for enabling schools to succeed with all children, the interest of the dominant elite is to preserve its hegemony over schooling, which amounts to a denial of equal opportunity for all children (Brantlinger, 2003; Sapon-Shevin, 1994). Bourdieu was not the first sociologist or political scientist who observed this phenomenon.

Schooling is one of the many ways inequality is preserved. And resistance to changes in schooling, except for the so-called reforms that advance even more expressions of inequality (Anderson & Pini, 2011; Ravitch, 2010a), is fierce. The noted community organizer and social change agent Saul Alinsky (1971) wrote:

> All societies discourage and penalize ideas and writings that threaten the ruling status quo. . . . From the haves . . . there has come an unceasing flood of literature justifying the status quo. Religious, economic, social, political, and legal tracts endlessly attack all revolutionary ideas and action for change as immoral, fallacious, and against God, country, and mother. (p. 7)

Parenti (1978) added to this by saying that the ruling classes represent their interests and wrap them in the *sacranda*, the basic sacred symbols of a nation's identity. "The interests in an economically dominant class never stand naked," he noted. "They are enshrouded in the flag, fortified by the law, protected by the police, nurtured by the media, taught by the schools, and blessed by the church" (p. 84).

Bourdieu (1998) explained that educational systems have their own rules of logic but that, while persons connected to those systems may not always be rational or even right to make the decisions they do, "they may engage in behaviors one can explain, as the classical philosophers would say, with the hypothesis of rationality, without their behavior having reason as its principle" (p. 76).

What this means is that there is a logic at work within a field of practice such as education, but it doesn't have to be logical outside the system in which it is located. It also means that for one to understand how to change educational practice successfully, one must first understand the implicit logic behind a practice, without expecting it to be logical. At the heart of this nexus is the fact that Bourdieu seriously questioned whether a disinterested act was even possible for those within or in charge of, practically or politically, national educational systems.

WHO BENEFITS FROM SCHOOLS AS THEY ARE?

A useful way to examine schools and what they actually do in the larger social space is to apply Blau and Scott's (1962) maxim of "cui bono." This means asking, "Who is the primary beneficiary" in maintaining or changing the workings of educational systems (p. 42)? Answering the "cui bono" query rests on accurately perceiving how educational systems really work and who actually benefits from them. It is clear that educational systems work best for the most economically well-off and that they have never been especially effective for children of the poor (Heymann, 2002). According to Bourdieu, this is not an accident.

Most experienced teachers and educators who have worked with children have confronted the same phenomenon. Some children and their parents have a difficult time learning school expectations. Sometimes the attitude of a child and/or his or her parents directly opposes or at least seems indifferent or antagonistic to the school's expectations. These may be class based, as in the case of females within certain social groupings who are not expected either to excel or to go into higher education, or based on religion, as one of the authors of this book (F. English) learned when he taught a science class with a Christian Science student who had to be excused from the room whenever germ theory was discussed.

Sometimes dispositions and perspectives regarding schooling are spread across an entire group of individuals, which Bourdieu referred to as "a collective habitus." Rothstein (2004) cites evidence of such a condition, based on a report from the International Association for the Evaluation of Educational Achievement (Turney-Purta, Lehman, Oswald, & Schulz, 2001):

> The inability of schools to overcome the disadvantage of less literate home backgrounds is not a peculiar American failure but a universal reality. The number of books in students' homes, for example, consistently predicts scores within almost every country. Turkish immigrant students suffer from an achievement gap in Germany, as do Algerians in France, as do Caribbean, African, Pakistani, and Bangladeshi pupils in Great Britain, as do Okinawans and low-caste Buraku in Japan. (Rothstein, 2004, p. 20)

For Bourdieu, the education system plays a crucial role in reinforcing any existing habitus and building new habitus. School systems build on and reinforce habitus from family experiences by providing a structure for inculcating an understanding and acceptance of the prevailing social "rules." The school system possesses what is termed a "transposable, durable habitus," whereby the habitus and associated "learning" are sustained well beyond the period of training. However, this training can either reinforce or conflict with the training brought by different social groups or classes. It is therefore understandable that some groups find the school's habitus "proper," understandable, and reinforcing, while other persons from different groups find it puzzling, alienating, and contentious.

ILLUSIO AND UNQUESTIONED LOYALTY TO CONTINUING ORTHODOXIES

The educational system seeks to instill in its participants an awareness of the "rules of the game." Schools do not exist only to impart technical knowledge and skills but also, importantly, to transmit "socialization" into a particular cultural tradition by building the understanding of the "rules of the game" to the point where this understanding seems almost "natural." In the previous chapter, we noted that Bourdieu (2000) called this understanding doxa, "a set of fundamental beliefs which does not even need to be asserted in the form of an explicit, self-conscious dogma" (p. 16).

All social fields have prevailing modes of thought and belief content, as well as generally accepted remedies for an array of problems, which keep being employed whether they are effective or not. Yet such remedies are believed to be basically true and necessary if there is to be any chance of success.

However, a simple awareness of the rules of the game would not necessarily be sufficient by itself to perpetuate the prevailing habitus within the existing social spaces or structures. This is because even though we might know the "rules," we might also choose not to "play," and in that case, the reproducing effects of habitus could be less potent. Bourdieu also argued that in addition to knowing the rules, there must be a willingness to adhere to them. He termed this state **illusio**, "the belief not only in the stakes, but also in the game itself, the idea that the game is worth the candle, that it is worth playing" (Bourdieu, 2004a, p. 50).

Earlier we reported data from a U.K. study on how family attitudes toward science actively work to shape the value children in those families place on a career in science (Archer et al., 2012). That research also indicated that family social class, as expressed in the interplay between capital and habitus, worked to make science either "thinkable" or "unthinkable."

However, even in working-class families where science was "unthinkable" and parents did poorly in that area of their own schooling, the researchers did not find that parents devalued schooling in general; that is, the "lack of science capital and the absence of science within the family habitus . . . did not equate with a 'poverty of aspirations' or a lack of valuing of education among the families" (Archer et al., 2012, p. 901). Thus, the *illusion* of learning and valuing science remained even when there appeared to be a realization that it wasn't for them.

It is perhaps the case that we often don't like the rules but go along with them either to "fit in"—for example, by following a dress code—or when we worry about the consequences of not playing by the rules; for instance, we might be tempted to fight with someone in the schoolyard, but we are less likely to do so if we know we will get in trouble for it. Therefore, we tend to comply with both the written rules, such as the law, and the unwritten rules, such as social conventions; thus, the status quo prevails.

The habitus includes both the overt ways of learning to be human within a specific social field and the covert or unwritten expectations and rules. One of the simplest manifestations of habitus is how children show respect for their elders. In some cultures, respect for elders is shown in the manner of addressing them as "sir" or "ma'am," with the eyes downcast and/or with a slight bow, as in Japanese society. In other cultures, respect for one's elders is shown by looking them straight in the eye and grasping their hand firmly. It is easy to get crosswise as an individual moves from one culture to another and continues to exhibit those behaviors and phrases of speech that enable him or her to move within one culture but are dramatically out of place in another culture.

THE BOUNDED NATURE OF CHOICE WITHIN A DESIGNATED SOCIAL SPACE

Most of us would argue that we have some social freedom of choice. We are free to choose which schools to send our children to; we can help them select some of their subjects or extracurricular activities and maybe help them with their homework. Yet the choices we make are bounded by what is *thinkable* within our own habitus, and because habitus works unconsciously, the limits are sensed but also invisible.

Bourdieu (1984/2009) also noted that within such designated social spaces people will adjust their life chances and bring their aspirations in line with the expectations of their particular social structures. Therefore, even where we perceive choice and actively engage in effecting influence in our children's education, we do so only in terms of what we perceive as being possible, or what is "thinkable," without ever considering that only some ranges of possibilities are permitted (see Reay, 2004, p. 433).

Within this social space, various social groupings work to control the school's agenda to advance and legitimate their own social positions. Brantlinger (2003), borrowing Bourdieu's notion of habitus, commented:

> Given the prevalence of school hierarchies and their resistance to change, it is reasonable to hypothesize that existing structures and practices are durable precisely because they correspond to influential people's desires, hence from their power to create and retain them. (p. 2)

She concludes that, "in reality, educational circumstances are not equal; wealthy white children inevitably are advantaged" (p. 2).

This phenomenon is apparent in the following example. With the exception of Asians as a subgroup, recent statistics on high school graduation rates in the United States support Brantlinger's (2003) assertion.

High School Graduation Rates in the United States for the Class of 2009

Group	Percentage Graduation Rate
American Indian	53.1
Asian	80.5
Hispanic	63.0
African American	58.7
White	78.8
National average	**73.4**

NOTE: Information from the EPE Research Center (Lloyd, 2012, p. 32).

Bourdieu argued that there is a potentially "darker" side to this phenomenon, as maintaining the status quo also means that any prevailing social inequities will be perpetuated as well. Bourdieu talked of the means by which we tend to "accept" the rules of the game and conform to expected behaviors, and concluded that, in doing so, we effectively *legitimize* the existing structures and forms of power that exist in our social space. We see things as being "normal"; we accept social hierarchies and our position within society, and we take for granted that others may have more or less privileged positions than we do. We don't tend to question to any great degree those whom we see as being in authority.

EDUCATIONAL INEQUALITIES MUST REMAIN UNNAMED

The true nature of schooling inequality is rarely discussed in public policy circles. Bourdieu similarly noted that certain educational inequalities remained unnamed and "are always what is least mentioned when students are discussed and especially when students talk about themselves" (Bourdieu & Passeron, 1979, p. 28).

Some educational researchers today have called this phenomenon "white privilege" (Apple, 2004; Swalwell & Sherman, 2012). This label refers to the fact that wealthy White students attend schools that "reinforce their perceptions of cultural dominance" (Swalwell & Sherman, 2012, p. 24) and are unaware of how their gender, race, class, and language grant them social privileges. They are sometimes referred to as students who "live in a bubble" (p. 24).

Apple (2004) discussed race not as a thing, "a reified object that can be measured as if it were a simple biological entity," but as "a *construction,* a set of fully *social relationships*" (p. 75). Apple called attention to the "invisibility of whiteness" and suggested that "those who are deeply committed to antiracist curricula and teaching need to place much more of their focus on white identity" (p. 80). Another example is that, when race is discussed, "race as a category is usually applied to 'non-white' people. White people are usually not seen and named. They are centered as the human norm" (p. 81). Dyer (1997) posited:

> The point of seeing the racing of whites is to dislodge them/us from the position of power, with all of the inequities, oppression, privileges, and sufferings in its train, dislodging them/us by undercutting the authority with which they/we speak and act in and on the world. (p. 2)

Effectively, then, social agents might be treated as inferior or have limited aspirations or opportunities for social mobility; yet such an imbalance is accepted as being "the way of things."

Prier (2012) analyzed the Race to the Top educational initiative of the Obama administration and called it a program that reaffirms "whiteness,"

> exposes the supposed "cultural deficits" in learning and academic achievement of persons of color, and awards and penalizes disparities between affluent and nonaffluent school systems, already dispropor-tionately segregated along racial and socioeconomic lines. (p. 12)

Prier (2012) insisted that the logic and priorities of No Child Left Behind (NCLB) in the United States "discount altogether the public good for persons of color in urban schools," because in an echo of Bourdieu's concept of habitus, NCLB "renders invisible the different sociocultural contexts that shape different lived experiences of diverse communities, who may in consequence produce different—not inferior—kinds of knowledge" (p. 16). Within this logic, NCLB is seen as "vintage whiteness," embedded in what Leonardo (2007) has termed "tough love and harsh sanctions" (Prier, 2012, p. 16).

CONNECTING THE DOTS: THE IMPORTANCE OF FAMILY IN SCHOOL SUCCESS

The home environment is the crucible where human beings acquire their habitus, those conscious and unconscious dispositions that are durable and transposable to other settings. Dumais (2006) examined data from the Early Childhood Longitudinal Study, collected by the U.S. Department of Education's National Center for Education Statis-tics in a file that contains 17,212 cases and information from parents and teachers. She reported that "support was found for Bourdieu's argument that families from different social class positions transmit different types and quantities of cultural capital and habitus to their children" (p. 102).

The family structure is where children learn what their "place" is in society. They learn to value certain forms of culture that are highly prized in the school and supported by the educational standards of the state, even if they find them remote, unreal, and ultimately unattainable.

—AERA

Twenty-one years before Dumais's (2006) article, Jeannie Oakes (1985) used Bourdieu's cultural reproduction theory in her work on the negative impact of tracking students in schools, remarking:

> The high-status knowledge, biased in favor of the middle class, serves to assign students from lower-class backgrounds to lower-status positions. Whether this high-status university-access knowledge is viewed as a limited commodity or as already under the "ownership" of the middle and upper classes, the result is the same; the existing society is reproduced. (p. 200)

Since Bourdieu and Passeron's 1979 sociological analyses and their affirmation of the family in attaining school success, additional empirical studies have validated their premises (Archer et al., 2012; Baker, Goesling, & Letendre, 2002; Buchmann & Hannum, 2001; Chiu, 2007; Chiu & Khoo, 2005; Chudgar & Luschei, 2009; Hanushek & Luque, 2003).

The intersection within the family of the concept of habitus and the forms of cultural capital relationally linked to economic capital and symbolic capital find their nexus in the family or "family habitus," as previously reported in the research of Archer et al. (2012). Different ethnic groups also configure the forms of capital differently (Aschbacher, Li, & Roth, 2010; Gilmartin, Li, & Aschbacher, 2006).

For example, one immigrant group that performs as well as or better than the White population is Asians. Asians are the fastest-growing highly educated population in the United States. "The number of Asians in the U.S. quadrupled between 1980 and 2010 to about 18 million, or 6% of the total population" (Jordan, 2012, para. 2). As a group, Asians place more value "on marriage, parenting, hard work and careers" (para. 3), and "three fifths of Asians say American parents don't put enough pressure on their children to succeed in school" (para. 18). The image that has emerged of Asian mothers, called "tiger moms," pushing their children to succeed is epitomized in a book written by a Singapore mom who took her children out of gym classes and school recesses because they were a waste of time ("Losing Her Stripes?" 2012, p. 49).

We have also seen in the case of gypsy families in the United Kingdom that some durable aspects of their culture are dead set against being transposed, because this group fears cultural assimilation and erasure. Their refusal to abide by school rules and "adapt" continues to result in appalling dropout rates and illiteracy levels among this lowest-achieving segment of the European population.

EST
paper
"at high
achievm
Black
girls

Gypsy culture is not the only one that actively opposes and resists the dominant school culture. Fordham and Ogbu (1986) documented how some Black students who did try to perform well according to the norms of school culture were either ostracized or assaulted by their Black peers. Solomon (1992) studied forms of resistance to White culture adopted by Black West Indian males in Canada. Solomon flatly declared that "black students in white dominant school structures have not benefited from Canada's policy of multiculturalism" because, "despite this national policy, dominant-group educators continue to embrace an ethnocentric approach to pedagogy within schools" (p. 125).

There was a tendency, according to Solomon (1992), for some educators to define such resistance as a kind of group pathology for which a variety of treatments were tried. According to this mind-set, "the emancipatory function of the black students' militant posture and group solidarity can easily be invalidated 'if they are seen as pathological behaviors'" (daCosta, 1978, p. 6).

THE CHALLENGE OF REDUCING SOCIAL INEQUALITY AS AN EDUCATIONAL GOAL

Public school personnel who are concerned with creating a more level playing field for the success of all children and for the betterment of the whole of a democratic society have to find ways to function within a system that has largely abandoned the social welfare ethic that worked to fund and staff good schools for everyone.

In considering change, educational leaders are confronted with an often perplexing array of situations and contradictions. Bourdieu's work provides not only solace but conceptual clarity for the conflict that has for some time been the hallmark of the need to improve schools in the United States and United Kingdom.

Kumashiro (2008) provided some good advice about this dilemma as he prepared student teachers to work using an approach he termed "anti-oppressive education," which Bourdieu and Passeron (1970/2000) identified as "the cultural arbitrary" (p. 23).

> I asked them [the student teachers] whether anti-oppressive teaching is something that happens only when all of the complexities are known, when all the contradictions are prevented, and when all the weaknesses are addressed. Was it a problem, in other words, to require that teachers come to a full understanding of oppression and

teaching before they feel comfortable teaching anti-oppressively? Was it a problem to define anti-oppressive teaching as only those instances of teaching that were not, in some ways, problematic? Some of the theories that we read in class suggested that anti-oppressive education is not something that happens when the contradictions and partialities are gone, but instead is exactly what happens when we are working through these "problems." (Kumashiro, 2008, p. 87)

The intention is not to create an impression that we as educators are dealing with a lost cause in which nothing we do will have any positive impact on our learners at all. Echoing the earlier discussion of habitus, which Bourdieu emphasized "was not a destiny," we also emphasize that Bourdieu's work offers us a set of "thinking tools" that enables us to review and reflect on our own practice and approaches, and to think about them in differing ways. These tools will be the subject of the chapters that follow.

IMPLICATIONS FOR POLICY AND PRACTICE

The relationship between the school and the larger social system is not a casual or random one. While many sociologists and other researchers have unmasked schools as essentially conservative social institutions and reproducers of existing social hierarchies (Bowles & Gintis, 1976; Willis, 1977), Bourdieu's approach recognized this feature but placed schooling in a larger social arena that was dynamic and intentional without having an expressed intent of necessarily being so.

One way to bring most of the concepts in this chapter together is to consider the impact of family on school success. In 1979, Bourdieu and Passeron summarized the importance of family by noting, "In the present state of society and of pedagogical traditions, the transmission of the techniques and habits of thought required by the school is first and foremost the work of the home environment" (p. 73).

KEY CHAPTER CONCEPTS

This section lists those ideas, concepts, and constructs that are most important to understanding Bourdieu's writing and his contribution to education. There is an entire corpus of sociologists and other experts who are worthy of additional reading. We have listed some of them here.

habitus

Perhaps no other concept is so connected to Bourdieu (1980/1990a) as the idea of *habitus*. A person's habitus encompasses those dispositions or "conditionings associated with a particular class of conditions of existence" (p. 53) that predispose a person to view reality in certain ways and not in others, without necessarily being conscious of them and without having been formally taught or directed in those ways.

An excellent review of this concept can be found in Chapter 5 of *Culture and Power: The Sociology of Pierre Bourdieu* (Swartz, 1997, pp. 95–116). Swartz explained in some detail how Bourdieu confronted the individual/society dualism by taking the position that "social reality exists both inside and outside of individuals, both in our minds and in things" (p. 96). Swartz noted that Bourdieu's concept of habitus shifted over time, from an early notion that it had a "normative and cognitive emphasis to a more dispositional and practical understanding of action" (p. 102).

In Chapter 3 of *Pierre Bourdieu: Key Concepts,* Karl Maton (2010) deals with the ambiguity of Bourdieu's concept of habitus, which is "one of the most misunderstood, misused and hotly contested of Bourdieu's ideas" (p. 49). Maton provides a formula to explain that [(habitus)(capital)] + field = practice. The formula shows that "practice" is the result of a person's (unconscious) dispositions (or habitus) and his or her position in the larger social space or field. This perspective highlights the relational nature of the concept of habitus.

field

A *field* is a social space. It is not empty or static but, rather, a *space of play* in which active social agents (players) vie with one another. Agents or players bring into this space certain dispositions, and they accept the rules governing their activities within this social space. These are the "rules of the game," many of which are not formally taught but are nevertheless learned, often unconsciously.

Field as a concept within Bourdieu's sociology is considered relationally with his notions of habitus and capital. One does not, for example, simply take the idea of a field and put various agents in it. A reasonable analogy might be the process of setting up a chess board. A chess board is only a chess board when what the pieces can do individually and relationally are simultaneously considered. Chess is not chess without chess pieces. Each piece has certain powers (or moves), and these may be compared to forms of capital. Thus, chess is a good example of relationality.

The major difference between Bourdieu's social space and chess is that a person's influence or power is not absolutely defined or confined but, rather, remains fluid. It would be like the knight or bishop in chess taking on larger or smaller moves (power or influence) as the game was played. Actually, if a longer time period is considered, spanning many chess games and many years, the chess queen—now the most powerful piece on the board—was once not so powerful. As Yalom (2004) observed, "It should not surprise us that the chess queen's official transformation into the strongest piece on the board coincided with the reign of Isabella of Castile (1451–1504)" (p. 192). The other difference found in Bourdieu's field is that the "moves" of the pieces are acquired unconsciously but understood by all.

A good reference for the concept of field is Patricia Thomson's (2009) chapter in *Pierre Bourdieu: Key Concepts*. Also, Loic J. D. Wacquant's (1992) chapter in *An Invitation to Reflexive Sociology* is excellent material for additional reading.

cultural arbitrary

Culture is a human construct. It is a system of arbitrary signs and symbols that are connected to "relations of domination and hierarchy, symbolically expressed and socially reproduced through the high, but arbitrary, valuation of upper-class culture" (LiPuma, 1993, p. 17). Choosing among cultures or cultural expressions is an exercise in power, since there is nothing intrinsically "better" about one form of culture among all possible cultures, past or present. Or, as Jenkins (2002) indicated, "other than as the result of an empirically traceable history, culture cannot be deduced or derived from any notions of appropriateness or relative value" (p. 105). Bourdieu's views on this are perhaps best expressed in his text with Jean-Claude Passeron:

> In any given social formation the cultural arbitrary which the power relations between the groups or classes making up that social formation put into the dominant position within the system of cultural arbitraries is the one which most fully, though always indirectly, expresses the objective interests (material and symbolic) of the dominant groups or classes. (Bourdieu & Passeron, 1970/2000, p. 9)

The importance of the concept of a *cultural arbitrary* in relation to school is that while the school provides social legitimacy to the selection of one specific culture over others, it is essentially an arbitrary act, though often cloaked in a form of false scientism regarding "best knowledge." Earlier in this chapter, we described past and present cultural and curricular controversies in the United States and United Kingdom. These disputes were resolved politically, not scientifically. The creation in the United States of the Common Core curriculum standards is a political act intimately connected to forms of culture (Gewertz, 2012; Jobrack, 2012). As such, it will serve to reinforce the educational inequalities that already exist in schools.

For an excellent synopsis of the cultural arbitrary and related concepts, see the chapter "Symbolic Violence and Social Reproduction" in *Pierre Bourdieu* (Jenkins, 2002, pp. 103–127).

illusio

This term is used in relation to a person's determination to participate in a field, obey its rules, and believe in its goals and objectives, becoming an active agent within that field. *Illusio* refers to the illusions that are part of the "rules of the game" of living and working within a field. It involves the acquisition of titles, prizes, salary, rewards, titles, and trophies but also the active pursuit of these things. As Bourdieu (1990b) observed, "social functions are social fictions" (p. 195), and the notion of illusion means that individuals work to fulfill their social function and thus take their place in the game.

3

The Curriculum, Qualifications, and Life Chances

WHAT THIS CHAPTER IS ABOUT

The selection of curriculum content is an expression of culture that is itself an arbitrary construct, meaning that there is no value-free curriculum. Since social power is continuously contested within a social field, the struggle over curriculum content is important, as the training delivered via schools can shape what is valued or not and what is understood by social structures. Thus, all forms of capital are apparent in education and are expended to retain and advance social status and power. The state assumes the role of arbiter of the struggle over curriculum, and its recognition provides legitimacy for the interests aligned with specific curricula, as well as the standards and tests that assess them.

School leaders should not view this struggle as one of "right" versus "wrong" but, rather, as a political struggle in which one group wants to maintain or advance its influence and domination over other groups. This struggle is often masked as one of "rigor" versus "more or less rigor," and the argument is often "won" by whichever curriculum produces the best test scores. We can see this argument used in the debate over the Common Core curriculum standards in the United States. However, tests themselves are not neutral indicators, as some are more aligned than others with specific curricula (English, 2010). So test scores cannot be the ultimate and final word on curricular propriety or selection.

When a specific curriculum is adopted, sanctioned, and enforced by the state, it represents a form of symbolic violence. This is because it involves the imposition of an arbitrary set of symbols and constructs on all other groups in the social space governed by the school. The domination of one set of curriculum content over all others is usually presented as normal, natural, or even inevitable.

As a state agency, most public schools are the means of retaining the advanced social standing of some groups over others, achieved in part by the sanctioning of some curricula and the exclusion of others. In this way, the school is a means of retaining the social control of some groups at the expense of other groups. School leaders must see this struggle for what it is as it plays out every day in many classrooms and must understand the stakes involved. There is no "scientific" or "neutral" way to resolve this struggle. It is normally resolved via political imposition, with the selected curriculum presented in a variety of ways as a matter for "experts," in an effort to try to conceal or disguise the arbitrary nature of the process.

Some children will always be much more familiar with the adopted curriculum than will other children because curriculum represents a symbolic system reflecting the dominant values of the dominant group. Thus, subordinate groups will necessarily always be at a disadvantage. To the extent that tests and curricula represent the values of the dominant group, there will always be an achievement gap, as illustrated in Chapter 2. Using the achievement gap as an excuse to further impose dominant group values on subordinate groups is a classic case of misrecognition, which will be discussed in the next chapter.

Specifically, this chapter addresses the following points:

- The school curriculum as a form of symbolic capital works to reinforce existing social hierarchies and is ultimately translated into economic capital advantage for the children of the more privileged classes.

- As a form of symbolic and cultural capital, the curriculum, when imposed on all children as an educational requirement, becomes a matter of symbolic violence. This creates, among other features, the so-called achievement gap in schools. Such gaps are likely to be a permanent feature of schooling until the true nature of their cause is understood.

- Neither curricula nor tests are culturally neutral constructs.

- Curriculum content struggles are contestations of a political struggle to preserve the social advantage of those in political power.

INTRODUCTION

Chapter 2 explored two of Pierre Bourdieu's core concepts, aspects of habitus and field. Here, the third of this trio of concepts, capital, will be considered, but we are reminded that these core concepts work together to influence many aspects of social life, including the schooling choices and curriculum content that act to determine the differing "values" placed on qualifications and education routes.

Bourdieu considered academic credentials to be significant, as qualifications are effectively translatable to economic capital, serving to reinforce mechanisms for social hierarchy and reproduction. This is because variations in access to different forms of education, including the curriculum design, can result in "unequal" chances for children. Hence, we will explore aspects of curriculum against Bourdieu's concepts as an example of an institutionalized educational mechanism that can be influential in determining children's academic progression, and an example of how culture and habitus play a role in their function.

Disputes over curriculum rigor have been, in part, the result of international test score comparisons based on the belief that national school systems can be objectively compared one to the other. Such comparisons are deceptive and conceal the actual function of schools to reproduce the existing social order of social and economic domination and subordination. This chapter deals with how schools, through the formal and hidden curricula, determine educational qualifications, educational success, and, ultimately, life chances.

THE THREE FORMS OF CAPITAL

Bourdieu understood capital to exist in many forms. He referred to symbolic capital as anything that is recognized as being capital by a particular field or social group, thereby gaining legitimacy. However, this capital falls into three principle forms: economic, social, and cultural. The primary and most easily recognizable form is that of **economic capital**. Bourdieu (1986) argued that economic capital was "at the root of all other forms of capital" (p. 252) because its value is universal across social groupings and fields, and because economic capital effectively "buys" access to opportunities that allow further accumulation of wealth and power in all its forms, thereby affording the holder a privileged position of influence or power.

Bourdieu determined that all forms of capital are important, as they directly relate to power and thereby to social structures and relationships. Put simply, capital is an expression of power (Calhoun, 1995). As we have seen with his other concepts, Bourdieu had a tendency to keep refining and adding to his ideas of capital; so the boundaries of what constitutes capital become very blurred, leading to a "tendency to see power everywhere and, in a sense therefore, nowhere—an extreme diffusion of power that Bourdieu himself rejects" (Swartz, 1997, p. 79). Therefore, rather than pursue the multifarious definitions derived by Bourdieu, we will focus on his central idea of symbolic capital, which he defined as

> any property (any form of capital whether physical, economic, cultural, or social) when it is perceived by social agents endowed with categories of perception which cause them to know and to recognise it and to give it value. (Bourdieu, 1998b, p. 47)

Essentially, as previously explained, capital is whatever is valued by a particular field or group within that field. Indeed, to be of even greater value, it would need to be recognized and prized between fields as well as within them.

While economic capital is the primary form of capital, the second form is **social capital**. This refers to all those social connections and networks that bring the old adage of "not *what* you know but *who* you know" to the fore, as social contacts can open doors and ease the way for accessing different social positions and opportunities that might not be open to those agents lacking such elevated levels of social capital.

EMPIRICAL VALIDATION OF THE IMPACT OF SOCIAL CAPITAL ON SCHOOL SUCCESS

Empirical support for these claims was recently proffered by a 2008 U.S. study of the utility of parental social capital, involving 25,000 eighth-graders derived from a 1988 National Education Longitudinal

Study database (Ream & Palardy, 2008). *Social capital* was defined as "the capacity of individuals to command scarce resources by virtue of their membership in networks or broader social structures" (Portes, 1998, p. 12).

Using concepts derived from Bourdieu's (1986) perspective—that is, that the reproduction of certain forms of power and privilege is associated with the inequitable distribution of social capital to various social groups—the study affirmed that "race and class characteristics are interwoven to the disadvantage of minority groups" (Ream & Palardy, 2008, p. 250).

While this study illustrated Bourdieu's notion that forms of capital are relational and not always convertible one to one, there was one exception. That exception pertained to the test scores of middle-class children, who were in an excellent position to prosper from their parents' knowledge of how to influence school practice and policy. In a trenchant summary of this research, Ream and Palardy (2008) commented, "We find that parents at higher rungs of the social class ladder are characterized not only by disproportionate wealth and know-how, but also by more bountiful stocks of what counts for this study as parental social capital" (p. 255).

THE POWER OF CULTURAL CAPITAL AND BOURDIEU'S OWN EXPERIENCE AS A STUDENT

The third form of symbolic capital is **cultural capital**, a noneconomic, largely intangible, and difficult-to-measure form of capital that is represented in manners, taste, bodily deportment, dispositions, dress, consumption patterns, and forms of knowledge that are approved—or not approved—by the school and its agents.

The great effort of students from lower social origins to overcome obstacles in school is often not enough to make up for the cultural capital they lack. This is not a new finding. For example, more than 30 years ago, Dimaggio (1982) showed that in the case of 2,900 eleventh-grade boys and girls, "the impact of cultural capital on high school grades . . . [was] 'very significant'"(MacLeod, 1987, p. 100), with those students who possessed cultural capital more similar to the school's getting much better grades.

It is interesting to note Bourdieu's recollections of his own lack of cultural capital in his educational experience. As a child from one of the poorer families in his region, he was acutely aware of how his dress reflected on himself and his family as being inferior to his more affluent classmates. "I lived my life as a boarder in a kind of stubborn fury," he reflected, which "made no small contribution to my revolt against the punishments and persecutions imposed by the petty officials whom the very norms of scholastic life led one to despise" (Bourdieu, 2004b, p. 96).

Later, Bourdieu (2004b) recalled those "monotonous regularities" of boarding school that were the result of the

> routine of everyday anxieties and struggles, all the calculations and ruses that had to be deployed, at every instant, to secure one's due, keep one's place, defend one's share . . . arrive on time, win respect, always ready to exchange blows, in a word, to survive. (pp. 92–93)

Young Bourdieu was marked by school officials as a "discipline problem." He received punishments and detentions—he estimated as many as 300 in his school career—and he lamented that as an adult he did not know how to give the child who had endured this ordeal of "despair and rage, his longing for vengeance" (Bourdieu, 2004b, p. 93).

SCHOOLS AS INSTITUTIONALIZED EMBODIMENTS OF FORMS OF CULTURAL CAPITAL

Cultural capital extends to education as the "cultural" understanding and appreciation that gives access to different areas of society, and includes educational institutions that are viewed as holding various levels of esteem. This is a form of cultural capital that is "institutionalized" and where educational credentials, or qualifications, awarded by different educational institutions hold different levels of "prestige" and therefore value.

For example, while the actual differences may be small or nonexistent, a degree from Stanford University is generally held in higher esteem than one from Montclair State University. The higher esteem accorded to Stanford constitutes a form of symbolic capital that is translatable to economic capital, in that the "right" education and qualifications can command a higher capital value and afford access to higher-earning employment opportunities. However, this capital is not evenly distributed in the social field, nor is it equally accessible to all social agents.

Indeed, schools have the capacity to reinforce and confer different forms of capital on their participants—for example, in terms of qualifications or an appreciation of "good" art and literature. This will reinforce which friendship groups are "appropriate" and what ways to behave are "acceptable" and, importantly, what behaviors do not conform to this pattern. All such approaches serve to render school an important means of promoting compliance to the prevailing social codes, by determining what is deemed acceptable and what is not.

These factors therefore play a key role in creating (and maintaining) social inequalities and reproducing social structures. The significance of education as a form of cultural capital and the importance of symbolic capital in accessing and recognizing this will be further considered in the following sections.

CAPITAL, POWER, SYMBOLIC VIOLENCE, AND SCHOLASTIC HABITUS

The importance of schooling is that it transmits patterns of the dominant culture that are mirrored in school curricula and other routines and that include the attendant master dispositions to value and extend those patterns. In this way, schools themselves play a focal role in imbuing their students with the prevailing culture and "rules" of society, which will be determined to a greater extent by those with more symbolic capital and, therefore, more symbolic power. These early educational experiences, both in school and in the way education is perceived within the family and social group, form a type of habitus—a "scholastic habitus"—that remains with us and influences our continued approaches to how we "value" education, how important we think it is to us, and what we consider an appropriate education. Here, habitus, coupled with cultural and social capital, plays an important role, as it is not merely a case of making the progression through the various levels of academia; it is also about selecting the "right" qualifications and academic institutions. This relates to early upbringing and education that forms a scholastic habitus—which, as previously explained, means the development of an approach to education and seeing it as having "value"—and leads to viewing some routes through education as being the preferred or natural choices.

Bourdieu and Passeron (1979) explained:

> Not only do the most privileged students derive from their background of origin habits, skills, and attitudes which serve them directly in their scholastic tasks, but they also inherit from it knowledge and know-how, tastes, and a "good taste" whose scholastic profitability is no less certain for being indirect. (p. 17)

From their habitus and the influences of symbolic capital, these "most privileged students" are better able not only to identify prestigious institutions but also to access them and to know the "right" subjects to study to gain access to the "best" schools and universities.

More children from families holding enhanced levels of capital view higher education as an accepted, unquestioned path than do children from families holding less capital. For these more privileged children, the choice of remaining in education appears more natural than, say, for children who need to find employment. As Bourdieu and Passeron (1979) indicated, "social origin exerts its influence throughout the whole duration of schooling, particularly at the great turning points of a school career" (p. 13).

Yet, given that not all of us can enjoy the same opportunities to access and benefit from education, it remains that some will be better placed to influence education policies and to determine the education choices that members of a field will receive. Indeed, it is unlikely that these privileged agents would either instigate or support any reforms that would bring about radical social change, because they would not support anything that might undermine their own elevated position brought by holding valued capital within that field. The controlling nature of capital and power constitutes **symbolic violence**, which Bourdieu (1972/1977) explained as being the "gentle, hidden form which violence takes when overt violence is impossible," rendering it a form of aggression that, because of the interplay with habitus, might not be recognized as such by those inflicting the violence or even the recipients of it (p. 196), as it is the accepted pattern of "the way things are."

TWO RECENT EXAMPLES OF SYMBOLIC POWER (VIOLENCE) IN SCHOOL CURRICULA

The idea of symbolic violence is not meant to suggest that we are all passive. Bourdieu's analyses of contestation in specific social fields revealed that even though members may be classified as having similar characteristics—such as their level of economic capital—jostling for position, protesting, and contesting policy, for example, remain integral features of any field. As explained in Chapter 2, social agents are not simply acquiescent, especially if their own positions of influence are involved, and Bourdieu (1993) strongly argued that fields comprise various forces and involve struggle between and among those forces. In other words, a field is never wholly homogenous but consists of a contested space with stratified social systems and hierarchies that tend to endure by being reproduced. This struggle for distinction or position is an ever-present feature of social life, making the issues of power and power relations fundamental.

One example is the creation and implementation of the Common Core curriculum standards in the United States. The Common Core movement began in 2006 when former North Carolina Governor James B. Hunt convened a meeting of a select group of educators and policy experts to consider creating national curriculum standards. After this gathering, papers from a variety of recognized scholars were commissioned to examine the impact of creating national curriculum standards. Following this, the Hunt Institute began shaping an approach to the formation of national standards.

The move was enhanced when the National Governors Association and Council of Chief State School Officers came together to forge a joint agenda. In 2009, a coalition of the National Governors Association, Council of Chief State School Officers, National Association of State Boards of Education, Alliance for Excellent Education, Hunt Institute, and Business Roundtable collaborated in the development of what is today known as the Common Core curriculum standards (Rothman, 2011). When the U.S. Department of Education made the implementation of the Common Core curriculum standards part of its Race to the Top initiative, more symbolic power was added to this movement with the endorsement of the federal government.

Leaving aside for the moment the exact nature of the content of the Common Core, Bourdieu spoke at length about how, within a contested social field and without any one agency holding absolute power, agents and agencies join together to forge what has been called a "world-making view." This master label consists of a categorically absolute symbol of authority and legitimacy. To possess such symbolic power and ultimately impose it, as has been the case with the Common Core movement, the master vision must be perceived as being based in reality and the groups advocating it must have sufficient symbolic capital to compel its recognition. Bourdieu (1990b) said it best when he wrote, "Symbolic capital is a credit, it is the power granted to those who have obtained sufficient recognition to be in a position to impose recognition" (p. 138).

The new Common Core curriculum standards are a wonderful example of a form of cultural capital at work, as embodied in a type of symbolic capital that has been elevated above all others. When a high school diploma is granted as being from a Common Core base, which, arguably, has been advanced on the grounds of its alleged superior "rigor," it becomes a kind of universal piece of cultural capital, and "as an official definition of an official identity, it releases its holder from the symbolic struggle of all against all by imposing the universally approved perspective" (Bourdieu, 1990b, p. 136). When symbolic capital becomes a kind of universal capital via collaboration in a contested social field, the result has been called "political power par excellence" (p. 138).

Another example of a different kind of symbolic power (and violence) in curriculum occurred when the Texas State Board of Education insisted that textbook writers not use the term *capitalism* but instead refer to "the free enterprise" system. Writers were also to refrain from using the word *imperialism*, instead substituting *expansionism*, a term deployed when dealing with U.S. territorial acquisitions (Frank, 2010). The Texas State Board of Education also erased Thomas Jefferson from the state curriculum because he was too secular. Gurwitz (2010) said of the board's decision, "What they accomplished isn't conservative. It's not pro-family, pro-life, pro-freedom or patriotic. It's idiotic" (p. 9B).

But what is missed in Gurwitz's assessment is that all curricula are social constructs based on one or more sets of what is valued and then accepted by the most powerful of social agents and agencies within the education field. The curriculum may have nothing to do with what is true or good. "Symbolic power is a power of creating things with words," observed Bourdieu (1990b), "a power of consecration or revelation, a power to conceal or reveal things which are already there" (p. 138).

Such legitimation and misrecognition of symbolic power essentially legitimize social hierarchies and permit those in dominant positions with more capital—or power—to control capital and effectively reproduce existing social structures, thereby maintaining the status quo.

SOCIAL ORIGIN AND SCHOOL SUCCESS: HISTORICAL AND CONTINUING EVIDENCE OF THE LINKAGE BETWEEN THEM

Bourdieu and Passeron (1979) argued that of all the differentiating factors in social relations, in education "social origin is doubtless the one whose influence bears most strongly on the student world" (p. 8), as both access to educational institutions and qualifications are in part determined by social status and can continue to determine a level of "success" that persists well beyond schooling. This is because, primarily, only those holding high levels of cultural capital can enjoy an education that carries with it opportunities for further privilege.

Thus, the educational system, access to various forms of schooling, and curriculum or qualification pathways play a central role in legitimating and maintaining these social structures via the "value" assigned to academic credentials and institutions, together with the definitions of what constitutes a "good" education.

An excellent historical example of this situation was provided by Labaree (1988) in his longitudinal study of Central High School in Philadelphia, whose constituents viewed a

> high school credential as an economic commodity that could be exchanged for status in the open market. The exchange value of this credential derived from its relative scarcity, which in turn derived in part from the high school's limited enrollment. (p. 50)

Labaree (1988) explained that the Central High School was based on both academic ability and social origins and therefore could fail even the wealthiest of students, but he stressed that while a bright working-class boy could possibly be admitted to the high school and a less academically able middle-class boy turned down, the actual probabilities were reversed.

A similar situation was reported in England, where Saunders (1996, as cited in Power, Edwards, Whitty, & Wigfall, 2003) indicated that private (fee-paying) schools were able to protect even "dull" middle-class children, as they were better able to get children "through examinations irrespective of their abilities or ambitions" (p. 44).

Bourdieu and Passeron's path-breaking 1979 research on social class and access to higher education pinpointed a startling fact—that the opportunity of obtaining a college education is the result of a selection process of the total school system and is available unequally depending on the student's social origin. "In fact, for the most disadvantaged classes, it is purely and simply a matter of elimination" (p. 2).

More than 40 years later, Carnevale's (2012) study of the 200 most selective colleges in the United States showed that students from the bottom income quartile accounted for less than 5% of the total enrollment in those colleges, about which Carnevale commented,

> In a society where people start out unequal, the test-based metrics that govern college admissions become a dodge—a way of laundering the money that comes with being born into the right bank account or the right race or ethnicity. (p. B8)

Kahlenberg (2012) similarly remarked that "instead of counteracting the inequalities they inherit, colleges and universities magnify them. Higher education in the United States is highly stratified, showering the most resources on the most-advantaged students" (p. B6).

Likewise, in the United Kingdom there are repeated criticisms of the low numbers of state school students accepted to the best universities, and repeated complaints in the popular press of the decrease both in numbers and in type of working-class children who attend meritocratic grammar schools (Shaw, 2013, p. 21). The increasing disparities of wealth in the United States and Britain are seen by many economists as a threat to the democratic welfare of both nations, and the educational policies of both are serving to increase those disparities (see Irvin, 2008).

ACADEMIC FAILURE AS THE "FAULT" OF THE STUDENT?

Indeed, when there is debate over university admissions or where some students fail to pass exams at the required level, the argument is often related to the students' own "failure" to exhibit ambition or aspiration in academic achievement or thinking about a future career. Such arguments can be seen in the earlier illustration of elite U.K. university entry as disproportionately divided between students educated in private and state schools.

In defending this situation and asserting that the universities are working hard to redress the imbalance, Wendy Piatt, the director general of the Russell Group of universities in the United Kingdom, stated that "this is an entrenched problem and there is no quick fix. It will take time to raise aspirations, attainment and improve advice and guidance offered to students in some schools" (Paton, 2013). She added, "We can only admit students who actually apply and who have the right grades in the right subjects" (Paton, 2013). These statements suggest that potential applicants lacked the aspirations to apply for prestigious universities and that even those who did perform well on entrance examinations were not necessarily skilled in the right subjects to gain admittance to the university. Thus, it was the students' "own fault" because they had failed to consider what prestigious universities require and made incorrect or unwise choices.

A recent Gallup poll of nearly 1 million U.S. students in Grades 5 through 12 during 2009 to 2011 revealed that student success in school was connected to having a positive outlook (Heitin, 2012). Bourdieu and Passeron (1979) observed the same phenomenon a little differently. They discerned that some students, by virtue of their social class position and its congruence with schooling expectations, "inherited" the existing school culture.

> But the culture of the elite is so close to the culture taught in school that a child from a petit-bourgeois background (and a fortiori from a peasant or working-class background) can only laboriously acquire that which is given to a child from the cultivated class—style, taste, sensibility, in short, the savoir-faire and art of living that are natural to a class because they are the culture of that class. For some, the learning of elite culture is a conquest paid for in effort; for others, it is a heritage, which implies both facility and the temptations of facility. (p. 24)

While Bourdieu cited lack of aspiration as a feature of some social groups, he did not associate this with student "failure" but, rather, deemed it a product of the uneven distribution of symbolic capital that existed in the larger social field and linked to habitus, with those people who start with less capital striving the least for advancement. This stems from a belief that they should be content with what they have, not due to any "failing" but because their ambition to achieve is confined by the limitations established by such things as their field position and background (see also Webb et al., 2002).

The implication of this state of affairs is that differences in power mean that competition for symbolic capital, in all its forms within a field, is uneven. Different groups will compete for different capital based on what they have realistic expectations of attaining. They will, in effect, self-impose boundaries on their ability to achieve successfully based on the limitations of their education, social connections, and position within the field. In this way, the mechanism for reproducing existing relationships is embedded in the structure itself.

ACADEMIC CREDENTIALS—ESSENTIAL CAPITAL?

The issue of what constitutes the "best" form of qualifications, what these qualifications are, and which are the most highly valued and transferable to other fields continues to be the subject of much debate. This debate has gathered pace, with an emphasis on a more instrumentalist ideology whereby education has a primary purpose of equipping people for work.

An example is found in the goal of making high school children "college ready" by graduation. This pursuit reflects a persistent emphasis on higher education as the most desirable means to secure employment and reinforces the tendency for nations to compare their own academic results against those of other nations, as if education itself is a competition in which it is assumed those nations with the "best" academic results will also be the most economically competitive.

Rotberg (2011) contested the assumption that international test scores are related to international economic competitiveness. For example, he made the point that arguments claiming a shortage of graduates in some areas, such as engineering, fail to account for those graduates who transfer to other employment areas rather than remaining in engineering, suggesting that the issue is not a national shortage of U.S. graduates but, rather, a case of employers being unable to hire graduates "at the wages they would prefer to pay and find[ing] it cheaper to out-source" (p. 32). Rotberg similarly pointed out that of the 30 occupations expected to exhibit the fastest growth, fully 53% do not require a college degree.

Thus, while the rhetoric highlights a quest for ever-improving test scores, with an assumed connection between test scores and economic competitiveness, there is an apparent disjunction between this perceived need and the actualities of the labor market. So why such an emphasis on producing "college-ready" high school graduates?

As Emery and Ohanian (2004) more bluntly put it: "You have to ask why the corporate elite is so hell-bent on pumping up the pool of skilled workers" (p. 20) in a time of unemployment when the highest job demand is found in those areas not requiring college degrees. They conclude that the "corporate fat cats" prefer a situation where "there are more highly skilled workers than there are jobs . . . [because] when you have lots of people competing for few jobs, workers are scared and compliant" (p. 20).

Emery and Ohanian (2004) argue that the burden of the cost of higher education borne by many students and their families is perhaps unnecessary. They question whether so many high school graduates should go to college when they may leave with a large debt and be unable to secure employment to pay it off. From Bourdieu's perspective, this could be seen as limited access to economic capital, thereby creating a barrier for those wanting to change their position either within a field or to a different field.

However, the emphasis of many U.S. state education departments continues to be placed on pushing test scores and perpetually measuring school success against prescribed attainment results, encouraging young people to remain in education to acquire the skills the authorities deem necessary for building economic competitiveness.

The language of the reformers and the groups pushing this agenda is totally absent of concerns regarding social inequalities and social justice. They see the schools as a means to an end that affirms their own position of dominance and enhances their control of education. For the moment, they appear to have achieved that end. To envision a different future, we begin with Bourdieu's (1991) observation: "To change the world, one has to change the ways of making the world, that is, the vision of the world and the practical operations by which groups are produced and reproduced" (p. 137).

THE HIDDEN CURRICULUM, CULTURAL VALUES, AND SCHOOL SUCCESS

That schools bestow values on their students via school culture and curriculum, for example, is generally accepted and, arguably, deliberately used to instill those attitudes and behaviors considered most desirable in members of society, especially by those defining the values to be instilled. It is not unusual to find curricula that purposely seek to influence behavior in such a way. For example, the citizenship and personal, social, and health education curricula in England and the character education curriculum in the United States purport to promote "positive habits or virtues," and it is common to find in such curricula references to moral education and equipping children to "take their place in society."

However, such efforts to influence behavior and values are not always so overt. Schools function in the dominant culture in which they are embedded. The close congruence between schooling and social expectations as embodied in law, customs, and cultural practices extends to both the formal and public curricula but also appears in the informal and **hidden curriculum** (Eisner, 1992). The hidden curriculum represents the cultural content that is not consciously thought about but that, through school routines, often represents unconscious assumptions and expectations.

Given the element of "concealment," it is perhaps inevitable that the role of the hidden curriculum in "controlling" a population has long been the subject of debate and theorizing, largely polarized between two views. One view, functionalism, argues that the hidden curriculum promotes the transmission of collective values where there is general consensus over what these values are. In this way, schooling contributes to the effective, smooth running of society. However, other writers focus on an approach that embodies more "conflict" and a more deliberate nature to this situation, suggesting that the purpose of education is to reproduce social structures in a way that keeps people in their place within the social hierarchy and to serve the needs of a capitalist or market-focused economy.

This argument, notably expressed in Bowles and Gintis's (1976) *Schooling in Capitalist America*, suggests that schools promote values such as obedience, punctuality, and discipline, making students work-ready and unquestioning and thereby maintaining the economic status quo. However, while others, including Bourdieu, would sympathize with elements of this argument, especially in serving social reproduction, Bourdieu did not consider people to be so docile or unquestioning. He understood that any group's culture was really its own take on the world and its place in the world. As he observed, "the members of different social classes differ not so much in the extent to which they acknowledge culture as in the extent to which they know it" (Bourdieu, 1984/2009, p. 318).

CALCULATING LIFE CHANCES: THE ACADEMIC VERSUS VOCATIONAL EDUCATION DEBATE

Concerns about what to do with children who encounter great difficulty in academic work plague both the United States and United Kingdom. In the United Kingdom, worries over labeling children and how this might hamper their progression were reflected in a report from the mid-1980s, which showed that students in the private schooling sector and the "best" secondary schools had the highest school-leaving examination scores. The authors of the study observed that advantage came from remaining in education and achieving higher qualifications, such as those at the A level (advanced level), the entry requirement for universities. Those students not achieving such qualifications might have been more likely to follow a vocational route by working and learning a trade, but they were at a disadvantage compared with those taking the more accepted route, as alternative, more highly paid professions were not open to them (Power et al., 2003).

Indeed, another author reported that, for both universities and employers, "almost any collection of A levels was preferable to vocational 'equivalents'" (Killeen et al., 1999, as cited in Power et al., 2003, p. 46).

That those groups holding the most power will seek to impose their influence to retain their preferential status is equally apparent in the way qualifications are discussed in terms of "value"—that is, which ones are the most desirable and which are effectively deemed second-rate. The significance here is that only those accreditations determined as holding value will be transferable between fields and, ultimately, translatable to economic capital.

In England, the question of which qualifications are the most prized was highlighted in a report by Professor Alison Wolf (2011) widely referred to as *The Wolf Report*. Wolf called for an overhaul of the vocational, or practical and technical, qualifications being offered in schools and colleges.

The use of the term *value* is significant here as a demonstration of how the field of power has the ability to affect the value of symbolic capital across many fields. Wolf (2011) reaffirmed the government's role in assigning value when she stated, "High quality vocational qualifications can and should be identified by the government, as part of its task of providing objective information to citizens" (p. 12). Here, the report legitimized the responsibility of the government in designating the value of qualifications by clearly identifying the government as the appropriate agency for deciding which qualifications will be offered.

From a Bourdieusian perspective, *The Wolf Report* similarly helped confirm the capital value of different awards, with the clear inference being that vocational qualifications hold a lower value than academic qualifications. Such assertions further elevated the position of the more "traditional" academic qualifications by establishing their superior value both within and between fields, thereby ensuring their dominant position and reproduction. Similarly, the report affirmed the government's role in using its position to establish this hierarchy of value in the wider society.

This stance was bolstered with arguments that change was necessary to protect both the integrity of the school league tables and to prevent young people from gaining qualifications that hold no value in terms of securing employment or recognition in different fields. Wolf stipulated, "Pretending that all vocational qualifications are equally valuable does not bring them respect. On the contrary, it devalues vocational education in people's eyes" (Paton, 2012, para. 9). This statement was reiterated by Education Secretary Michael Gove when he said, "For too long the system has been devalued by attempts to pretend that all qualifications are intrinsically the same" (Vasagar, 2012, para. 9).

THE MALDISTRIBUTION OF OPPORTUNITY

Bourdieu argued that the value of social and, particularly, cultural capital is not uniform either within or between fields, or in relation to qualifications. What is highly prized in one group or field might carry less value in another. The examples presented earlier reflect this variation in the comparison between vocational qualifications and the more highly prized academic qualifications. We may not be conscious of it, but we all have some notion of what we consider worthwhile or valued qualifications, and even in cases where qualifications are deemed of "equivalent" worth, we are bound to consider one more valuable than the other. This is important across social fields but even more so if we in education also assign value, consciously or not, to qualifications, as this can impact our perceptions of learners and other teachers alike, given that teachers will deliver a whole range of courses from vocational (or practical) to academic in settings that may still foster a qualification value hierarchy. This is especially pertinent when we remember Bourdieu's argument that capital equates to power, which is embodied in the resources that are valued within fields and where qualifications are transmutable to capital and therefore power.

Further, these resources are the various forms of capital "that can be created, accumulated, exchanged and consumed" (Swartz, 2010, p. 46). Capital, qualifications, and experience "buy" entry to a field, determine the starting point within it, and affect promotions, movement, and influence. Bourdieu further argued "that power finds expression in the mundane activities of everyday life. It operates at a tacit, taken-for-granted level on both cognitive and bodily dimensions of human society" (Swartz, 2010, p. 48).

This situation means that some differences in terms of capital are accepted as the "norm," a part of everyday life and society. This feature emphasizes the significance of value differences in qualifications, given that they represent a form of capital that is translatable to increasing economic capital with a more highly paid position, symbolic capital in terms of securing status, and social capital by securing valued social connections.

Those without access to these forms of capital can still achieve movement within a field but in a more limited capacity. Bourdieu and Passeron (1979) spoke of the value of academic degrees, diplomas, and all forms of credentials that, when attached to positions and not individuals, result in permanent differences. These differences, once established, mean that "relations of power and domination no longer exist directly between individuals; they are set up in pure objectivity between institutions, i.e., between socially guaranteed qualifications and socially defined positions" (p. 187). In this situation, "academic qualifications are to cultural capital what money is to economic capital" (p. 187). For example, in an academic field, a PhD might be regarded as valuable and therefore represent high currency within the field or "marketplace," meaning that "the holder no longer has to engage in a 'symbolic struggle' about position" (Gunter, 2002a, p. 13).

Bourdieu referred to symbolic power as inflicting a type of non-physical violence, as it allows forms of oppression to continue unopposed by, for example, categorizing social groups, setting education standards, and determining accepted social behaviors. Acceptance of the need for qualifications to teach certain subjects and/or academic levels or to work in different roles within education is an example of this practice, as it sets the boundaries for progression and access to capital depending on capital held. It is important to understand that capital is dependent on the value placed on it within the field and the value it carries in other fields, recognizing that what is highly valued in one field might not be so prized in another. "This means, concretely, that the social rank and specific power which agents are assigned in a particular field depend firstly on the specific capital they can mobilize, whatever their additional wealth in other forms of capital" (Bourdieu, 1989a, p. 123).

Thus, preventing access to qualifications or setting students on an early pathway to, say, vocational or less highly regarded qualifications can represent a "maldistribution of opportunity," as not all students will be afforded opportunities to access or acquire the academic credentials that confer greater cultural and symbolic capital; in this way, the existing dominant interests and structure of the field will be preserved and strengthened. As Bourdieu (1999) argued, deprivation of capital, in whichever form, "chains one to a place" (p. 127).

Discussions of school content rarely deal with the differences among policy, practice, and rhetoric. The rhetoric is often one of "reform." The practice mirrors the extension of the status quo. This is the case because the role of cultural capital is not neutral; it is present in the formal and hidden curricula and bestows compelling advantage and disadvantage on children from different social groups and backgrounds. The proposed curricular reforms in both the United Kingdom and United States are unlikely to change this situation to any meaningful degree.

IMPLICATIONS FOR POLICY AND PRACTICE

There is a strong and relational confluence of what schools teach in their curricula and which interests are represented in the content selected. All curricula are representational of the interests of some groups that are not necessarily the interests of other groups. Bourdieu saw school as a special social space that functioned as a symbolic space where different lifestyles competed with one another for legitimacy and primacy. In this sense, schools are pivotal locations of an often fierce flashpoint of political struggle. The parties in that struggle see their own values and perspectives as self-evident and good for everyone, and see opponents' questioning of these values and perspectives as subversive and conspiratorial. Proponents cloak their values in a mantle of self-righteousness, good manners, and good taste, and in the interests of the nation and the larger economic values that support their own wealth and continued prosperity.

Any school leader caught in the middle of a curricular content debate will recognize at once that this conflict, by nature, cannot be resolved by logic or appeals to an agenda of social justice—that is, decisions that reduce rather than perpetuate the existing nature of wealth disparity the school currently embraces and, in so doing, reproduces. Arguments must be carefully crafted to appeal to a broad democratic base and to avoid the "zero-sum game" antidote, which carries the perception that what other groups gain, "my group" must lose. Arguments must be framed as how all groups can "win" with the options presented.

The most telling question for leaders in the day-to-day operation of schools is, How much and how far can schools be recrafted so the interests of all are promoted without some being alienated and lost? This is a most compelling and complex issue. For example, while the recent international test score comparisons show that Britain has one of the finest educational systems in the world, that is true for only the very top percentage of students. For those children not doing well and who would not qualify for Britain's best universities (the so-called Russell Group),

> more than 13,000 children leave school at 16 every year with nothing to their name and as many again don't even go to the exams. . . . These are the children of the people of Britain and they have not been spoken for yet. (Collins, 2013, p. 17)

The key issue for policy developers is the question of how a monocultural curriculum that is most closely aligned with the interests and cultural family backgrounds of the existing group in control of s_ matters can be augmented to become more inclusive for all. Currently, the Common Core curriculum standards in the United States side-step this issue in the name of promoting increased "rigor," so as to fare better in comparisons of international test scores. What amounts to "rigor" in this case is simply an even more class-based artifact that will do nothing to decrease the already pronounced achievement gap based on race and economic condition. The nexus of these issues is the goal of somehow making curriculum and schooling more inclusive as opposed to exclusive.

KEY CHAPTER CONCEPTS

forms of capital

Bourdieu identified various *forms of capital* that individuals work to acquire and use to influence others in specific social fields. Those who have more capital are more powerful, and they exercise their influence to extend their reach, and certainly not to lose it. Other individuals or agencies want to acquire additional capital to expand their influence. The interaction that occurs takes various forms of contestation. Different fields have distinctive practices and follow their own logics and routines.

Thompson (1991) avers that Bourdieu employed the term *symbolic power* as an inclusive label to acknowledge "most forms of power as they are routinely deployed in social life" (p. 23). Symbolic power is felt by people in a field but often not clearly recognized for how it benefits some in the field more than others because it is in the end "an arbitrary social construction" (p. 23). School curriculum is a form of symbolic capital and, as such, is an expression of symbolic power.

Because curriculum revolves around cultural artifacts and shared cultural values, it works to enable some children over others to be much more successful in schools, primarily those children from the elite classes who by virtue of their political position use the schools as a means to retain their social and political power. Shared values are expressed as ideologies—that is, bundled beliefs regarding what is important, valuable, appropriate, and worthwhile, as well as the shared taboos about what is not.

We must remember that ideologies are always doubly determined, that they owe their most specific characteristics not only to the interests of the classes or class fractions they express (the function of sociodicy, but also to the specific interests of those who produce them and to the specific logic of the field of production. (Bourdieu, 1991, p. 169)

One of the key Bourdieusian ideas is that even those who find the culture embedded in school curricula to be unfamiliar or even antagonistic to their own values still must have a shared belief in its legitimacy. From this perspective, Bourdieu's insight that all the players in a social field have to share a common cognitive acceptance of it means that those who are least advantaged (or disadvantaged) participate in the perpetuation of their own inferior positions within the field.

These are the various forms of capital at work in a specific social space or field.

cultural capital

This concept refers to a process and a state of possessing certain forms of knowledge that have been acquired through an extended process, beginning in the family, and from which a person takes on certain tastes and values regarding cultural artifacts and forms in the larger society (see Lamont & Lareau, 1988).

In Bourdieu's work, *cultural capital* aligns with social structure (LiPuma, 1993, p. 18). The school incorporates the culture of the dominant classes and engages in a transformation of culture by classifying the dominant culture "as 'natural' talent, and thus 'natural' superiority, levels of knowledge among students which are in fact largely the result of an informal learning process taking place within the family" (Johnson, 1993, p. 23). Schools complete the process of legitimization as each "transforms social hierarchies into academic hierarchies, and, by extension, into hierarchies of 'merit'" (p. 23), and ultimately into social power. Thus, cultural capital can be converted into other forms of capital. "The example of cultural capital has demonstrated that signals of cultural knowledge are rewarded in the classroom, which is easily converted into a type of economic capital—educational attainment" (Robson, 2009, p. 107).

An excellent overview of cultural capital is provided in Randal Johnson's (1993) introduction to *The Field of Cultural Production* (Bourdieu, 1993). Another can be found in Edward LiPuma's (1993) chapter in *Bourdieu: Critical Perspectives*. Bourdieu's classic text is

Distinction: A Social Critique of the Judgment of Taste (1984/2009), a lengthy commentary on cultural capital and its homology to social position and social power.

economic capital

In the simplest terms, *economic capital* is money and material wealth. It is represented in the accumulation of funds in bank accounts, stocks, bonds, and in such things as the value of one's home, automobiles, jewelry, and other material acquisitions.

social capital

Bourdieu and Wacquant (1992) defined *social capital* as "the sum of the resources, actual or virtual, that accrue to an individual or a group by virtue of possessing a durable network of more or less institutionalized relationships of mutual acquaintance and recognition" (p. 119). Put another way, social capital is the influence one has or acquires via friendships and membership in groups such as fraternal or recreational (e.g., golf, tennis, poker, bridge) clubs, associations, or classes of like-minded persons in religious organizations or political parties.

symbolic violence

Linguistic exchange employs language as a symbolic system. Such exchanges occur between individuals and groups in a structured space, usually embedded in hierarchies of power. As such, linguistic exchanges are expressions of power and domination, and subordination. Social categorizations are based on linguistic expressions; certain expressions are sanctified as legitimate, while others are not. Legitimation of one over the other is the result of political struggle.

> Symbolic violence is thus a generally unperceived form of violence and, in contrast to systems in which force is needed to maintain social hierarchy, is an effective and efficient form of domination in that members of the dominant classes need exert little energy to maintain their dominance. (Schubert, 2008, p. 184)

The imposition of some linguistic systems over others is an act of symbolic violence, and it occurs when those in the dominant groups just go about their normal lives, enjoying living within the rules that perpetuate the world they rule.

hidden curriculum

The *hidden curriculum* is that part of the cultural content of schooling taught as part of the lived routines that make up systemized and state-sanctioned education. Eisner (1992) summarized the nature of the hidden curriculum as follows:

> The hidden curriculum consists of the messages given to children by teachers, school structures, textbooks, and other school resources. These messages are often conveyed by teachers who themselves are unaware of their presence. "Hidden" implies a hider—someone or some group that intentionally conceals. Concealment, in turn, suggests a form of subterfuge to achieve some gain. Hence, the hidden curriculum is often believed to serve the interests of the power elite, which the school itself is covertly thought to serve. (p. 314)

4

The Shifting Control of Leadership Preparation

❖ ❖ ❖

WHAT THIS CHAPTER IS ABOUT

The world is not "out there," existing in some pristine state and awaiting discovery. Rather, the world is an artifact, a creation and a construct of human symbols, the chief form of which is language. And language is intimately connected to culture. All the facets of culture are not obvious to those residing within it. Those living in a culture most often believe that their culture is "natural" and the way the world is and should be viewed. Aberrant versions and other cultures are often seen as intrusive, foreign, erroneous, repugnant, and/or outright evil.

A social field is just such a human construct, and it possesses its own logic of relationships and practice. Pierre Bourdieu's analyses show that education is one of those social fields. A social field is a social space containing individuals, agents, and agencies who reside there in a hierarchical, competitive, and sometimes contentious state, each vying to extend its sphere of influence and legitimacy. Legitimacy is obtained through forms of capital acquired by the players and through the formation of coalitions that seek to impose their specific vision of the world on all the inhabitants of that field. We review the impact of neoliberal or neoconservative ideas that Bourdieu opposed as they were introduced in France. However, the arguments used to advance neoliberal policies are very similar in the United Kingdom and the United States.

The histories of school leadership preparation in the United States and England show different temporal sequences. For example, Brundrett (2001) pointed out that "formal training for school leadership has been relatively rare outside the USA where university programmes for the preparation of school principals and superintendents can be traced back to the 19th century" (pp. 229–245). Such programs began in England only in the 1960s, "with the first chairs in educational management being established in the 1970s," and "by the 1980s taught higher degrees in educational management became an increasingly important part of the portfolio of university courses in England" (pp. 229–245). In the 1990s, there was "a growing acceptance that skills developed in the workplace should be seen as an integrated part of academic programmes" (pp. 229–245).

In her discussion of the creation of networks and networking among various agencies involved in knowledge production in the United Kingdom, Helen Gunter (2002b) observed,

> Knowledge claims about the interplay between the academy and practice are played out. In these spaces, meanings are created through position, and boundaries are contested through positioning. Illustrative of how the tensions and dilemmas facing the position and positioning of field members is lived in professional practice can be seen through how the academic-practitioner habitus has been simultaneously promoted and challenged. (pp. 7–26)

This chapter examines the field of logic and power in the preparation of educational leaders in the United States and the United Kingdom to show how the changing nature of leadership preparation portends dramatic changes in school site practices, but especially in the value orientation of school leaders. At stake is the ethic of public service versus the ethic of the marketplace and the idea of making education and schooling into a commodity (English, 2014).

Specifically, this chapter addresses the following points:

- Various ideologies in the United Kingdom and the United States advanced by neoconservative individuals or agencies are argued to have worked to extend their influence in school leadership preparation by deprofessionalizing it. Deprofessionalizing school leadership amounts to voiding licensure requirements and/or degree requirements from universities or colleges as a means to advance to school leadership positions in the field.

- The creation of leadership standards invariably involves reproducing the status quo as the means of validating them and amounts to the reification of existing practices along with freezing the inequities and inequalities that exist within schools. The standards, therefore, cannot be used to "reform" schools or substantially change existing practices or relationships.

- The professional educational social field remains fluid, dynamic, and strongly contested. Individuals and groups continue trying to expand their influence within the field to attain a position of hegemony. There is a constant struggle for domination and legitimacy.

- Reformers of educational leadership advance their agendas under the cloak of disinterestedness and try to mask the biases within it by appealing to the common good and common sense. Rarely do these agendas substantially diminish the social position of those advancing them. Disinterestedness is only a posture.

INTRODUCTION

Educational standards for leaders rest on assumptions regarding a knowledge base. Standards have to be seen as being founded on some more universal platform than merely one group's or person's biases about what leaders ought to be doing in schools. The knowledge base issue in the field of educational leadership in the United Kingdom and the United States is situated in the political positions of those who advance what counts as knowledge. The dominant groups bring with them prejudices regarding their own position and views about "otherizing" rival groups based on gender, race, or social class position. In short,

> understanding the production of knowledge requires an understanding . . . of how history can other women, bleach out issues of colour, privilege particular class distinctions (taste, deportment, and accent), and normalize particular ways of doing and being in the world and mask realities and preferences. (Gunter, 2006, p. 207)

Knowledge claims are part and parcel of an exercise in power. Foucault (1974) labeled this idea "power-knowledge," meaning that knowledge is never neutral and exists within a contested and hierarchical field. When institutions are involved, knowledge takes the form of an apparatus, leading to what Foucault termed a "regime of truth," where "truth is to be understood as a system of ordered procedures for the production, regulation, distribution, circulation, and operation of statements" (pp. 134–135).

The **field of power** is one of Bourdieu's most provocative and complex notions, which he applied rather extensively in his 1996 book *The State Nobility: Elite Schools in the Field of Power*. While this research was particularly focused on French education, much of the analysis is applicable to many other nations as well. In determining a field of power, Bourdieu began by mapping the relative positions in the field of various actors, agents, and institutions; how they impose or influence other agents or institutions; and the type of influence and capital acquired and expended in the process. We took Bourdieu's approach to education as a field of power in the United States and examined the major agents, agencies, and institutions through which graduates to educational leadership positions must pass to become licensed by the state to lead schools.

THE CONSTRUCTION OF NATIONAL LEADERSHIP STANDARDS IN THE UNITED KINGDOM AND UNITED STATES

The marginalization and/or erasure of competing voices and epistemological perspectives in the creation of leadership standards has followed very similar paths in the United Kingdom and the United States, ultimately embracing a culture of **managerialism** and neoconservatism in the former (Gunter & Thompson, 2010) and ruthless standardization (English, 2003) and neoconservative advocacy for the use of vouchers and charter schools (Giroux, 2004) in the latter. Indeed, the dominant ideology in both countries is represented in the neoconservative (aka neoliberal) agenda for commodifying public services, delegitimizing alternative epistemologies, and deemphasizing the efficacy of university preparation (English, 2006).

Gunter (2002a) noted that in England "the marginalization of HEIs [higher education institutions] is deliberate and part of a political concern to eradicate the humane and critical traditions of understanding experiences and meaning" (p. 90). In the United States, the Southern Regional Education Board (2006) said that "states and districts cannot depend on universities to change principal preparation programs on their own because the barriers to change within these organizations are too deeply entrenched" (p. 4).

We now discuss the hierarchical and contested nature of relationships in a Bourdieusian field, along with the abbreviated major intellectual steps involved in creating a set of national leadership standards in the

United States. A comparison of the development of standards in England and the United States shows similarities and differences. In England, "the National Professional Qualifications for Headteachers (NPQH), [was] predicated on a set of national competencies and taught not by professors, but largely by trainers" (Lumby & English, 2009, p. 108).

In the United Kingdom, three different periods spanning the years 1944 through 1988 were significant for the development of education standards, with the most serious criticisms and impacts of neoliberalism occurring from 1974 to 1988. Business management models "based on traditional hierarchical control enabled the headmaster tradition to be reworked into modern leadership behaviours and practice," which placed a premium on regulation and contractualism (Gunter, 2002a, pp. 21–23).

In the United States, the same tenets were crystallized into the new national standards for educational leaders, which were only tangentially part of the federal educational role. Because of the separation of power between state and federal governments that is embedded in the U.S. Constitution, the separate state departments of education incorporated the national standards into their licensing apparatus for principals and superintendents. Public and state tax-supported university and college departments of educational administration and leadership were made subservient to these standards via state and national (but not federal) accreditation reviews. Such reviews were part and parcel of the policing function, or what Foucault (1979), in his classic work, called "the normalizing gaze."

THE MAJOR EPISTEMOLOGICAL STEPS BEHIND NATIONAL STANDARDS

We will now review in some detail the major intellectual/epistemological steps for creating national standards in the United States. The first conceptual step was the extraction of a role within a hierarchy of roles in U.S. school systems. Principal (head teacher) is considered a middle-management position in the United States (Brown, 2005). The extraction process essentially freezes the role, because the logic of practice is centered on identifying the skills within an epistemology that erases the importance of context so these skills can become generic indicators.

The epistemology of the "performing school" in England is part and parcel of the vision of the efficient school in the United States and is deeply embedded in the Interstate School Leaders Licensure Consortium (ISLLC) standards.

To illustrate the prevailing similarities or parallels between the U.S. and U.K. systems, we will refer to their key features. The key features in England, as cited by Gunter (2002a), are listed below, followed by statements from the United States' ISLLC standards (in italics):

- "Education is a product and service to be marketed, bought, and sold, as the most efficient and effective way of organising and meeting consumer needs" (Gunter, 2002a, p. 18).

  The principal "uses effective marketing strategies and processes" (Hessel & Holloway, 2002, p. 77).

- "The purposes of schools and schooling are to enable the workforce to be appropriately skilled to operate in the current and developing economy" (Gunter, 2002a, p. 18).

  "The purpose of the Standards is to improve the performance of school leaders, thereby enhancing the performance of teachers and students in the workplace" (Shipman, Queen, & Peel, 2007, p. xiii).

- "Schools have stakeholders who invest their resources into learning outcomes, accountability is through measurement which enables judgments to be made about value for money" (Gunter, 2002a, p. 18).

  "The school leader identifies external forces that might challenge or support instructional programs and student achievement, communicates this information to the community, and collaborates to assess the impact of these forces and plans accordingly" (Hessel & Holloway, 2002, p. 111).

- "Leadership is about the location of entrepreneurial behaviours in the role and tasks of senior and middle management postholders" (Gunter, 2002a, p. 18).

  "A visionary leader must also do the following: attract commitment and energize people, create meaning in workers' lives, establish a standard of excellence, bridge the present to the future, and transcend the status quo" (Shipman et al., 2007, p. 15).

  "The effective leader assures that through this change process, appropriate curricular, co-curricular, and extra-curricular programs are designed, implemented, evaluated, and refined. Requisite resources for implementation are sought and, whenever possible, obtained" (Hessel & Holloway, 2002, p. 111).

- "Management systems in schools are designed to control and deliver education outcomes" (Gunter, 2002a, p. 18).

  "Applies appropriate models and principles of organizational development and management, including data-based decision-making,

with indicators of equity, effectiveness, and efficiency to optimize learn-
ing for all students" (Hessel & Holloway, 2002, p. 111).

"The school leader makes all management decisions in a way that
promotes the school's vision" (Shipman et al., 2007, p. 15).

- *"Teachers are the workforce to be trained and to be flexibly*
  trainable to deliver externally determined curricula by teaching
  through targets and testing" (Gunter, 2002b, p. 18).

"The school leader systematically collects and analyzes data on the
school progress toward realizing the vision. This monitoring and evalua-
tion must be tied directly to objectives and strategies demonstrating a
clear understanding of the link between effective teaching and student
learning, the school leader also regularly collects data on both student
achievement and teacher performance" (Hessel & Holloway, 2002, p. 61).

"The leader assumes that the areas in need of improvement will
have appropriate, measurable targets set indicating the increased
academic performance or achievement level anticipated" (Hessel &
Holloway, 2002, p. 64).

In the United States, the ISLLC standards embody the role of the
principal with similar partisanship:

Authors of current literature depict the administrator as the keeper of
the dream. The school leader is the creator of the dream and the driv-
ing force that moves the dream forward. The role of the administrator
is to manage the vision of the school. The role of the school leader is
to establish visionary leadership. Leaders initiate visionary leadership with an image of the organization for the future, shared among
stakeholders to grant empowerment and gain ownership and acceptance of a unified vision. Effective leaders inspire stakeholders, direct
the path to success, and assist the organization in dealing with
change. (Shipman et al., 2007, p. 10)

And the role of the teacher is cast as subservient, where "teachers
must examine current beliefs, develop a rationale for change, and
consider new models and strategies for school improvement" (Shipman
et al., 2007, p. 11). In addition, "to sustain credibility, the school leader
must embed the vision in the curriculum, staffing, evaluation, and
budget" (p. 34). And what of teachers who may be reluctant to be
embedded in the principal's vision? "To remedy the inability to embed
the vision into daily practices, principals must provide teachers with
continuous assessment, analysis, and professional development to
overcome the barriers of conceptualizing the vision" (p. 34).

CORE TECHNOLOGIES AND
THE REIFICATION OF THE STATUS QUO

The casting of managerial skills in England was similar to that in the United States, as not all the duties of principals were examined, only what was termed "the core technology." This distinction meant the elimination of "those dimensions of the job that traditionally have not been tightly linked to learning and teaching" (Murphy, Yff, & Shipman, 2000, pp. 17–40). As English (2000) pointed out, "the key to the idea of organizational rationality is embedded in the concept of a technical core" (p. 164). This perspective is also nicely aligned with the ideology of neoliberalism, or what Gunter (2002a, p. 17) has labeled "the performing school," and it has been advanced in both countries with a form of missionary zeal.

Core technologies have been described in the organizational literature for more than 40 years and are the hallmark of bureaucratic organizations. Close examinations of how core technologies are employed as extreme forms of bureaucratic rationality have also been provided in the literature—for example, by Thompson (1967), who observed that "perfection in technical rationality requires complete knowledge of cause/effect relations plus control over all of the relevant variables, or closure. Therefore, under norms of rationality, organizations seek to seal off their core technologies from environmental influences" (p. 24).

THE SHIFTING NATURE OF THE
CONTESTATION AND CHANGE IN
POWER IN THE EDUCATIONAL FIELD

Ever since educational administration was founded as an area of study in U.S. universities in the 1920s (Culbertson, 1988), the professoriate has been in a dominant position to define the nature of the logic of the field. While educational leadership roles had evolved in the schools prior to the initiation of courses and texts at the university, there was no intellectual legitimacy for them and certainly no formal preparation program for those desiring to become educational leaders. The establishment of the "field" of educational leadership occurred in the emerging schools of education, most notably at the elite private and public universities of the day, such as Teachers College Columbia, Ohio State, Harvard, and Stanford.

It remained for those occupying positions at the university to define the proper relationships among school administrators, the role of the school superintendent and its relationship to elected or appointed boards of education, matters of licensure to practice, the delineation of appropriate duties of midlevel managers (principals and supervisors) and school superintendents, and the proper orientation to work (think democratic vs. authoritarian forms of management). In those early times, the field was occupied by members of two major poles, the university professor and the school practitioner. Later, the national administrative associations were formed—for example, the National Association of Secondary School Principals in 1916 and the National Elementary School Principals Association in 1921. The oldest of these associations is the National Association of School Superintendents, organized in 1865 and now known as the American Association of School Administrators. At this time, the federal education effort consisted primarily of gathering national statistical data about schools, and little else. The federal Department of Education was not officially operational until May of 1980, following passage of Public Law 96-88 (Tallerico, 2006).

Since the inauguration of national accreditation in the 1950s and the increasing role of state departments of education in shaping licensure standards, the locus for definition of the function and role of school leadership has steadily shifted from the university to the state level. This shift in the field of power in educational leadership was accelerated by the development of the ISLLC, which created national standards to be used in accrediting university and college preparation programs via the National Council for the Accreditation of Teacher Education (NCATE) (English, 2000, 2003, 2006; McCarthy, 1999; Murphy, 1999; Murphy et al., 2000; Shipman et al., 2007).

Another development within the past 10 years is the entrance of what Ravitch (2010a) has called "the billionaire boys club," consisting of Bill Gates, Eli Broad, and others, and the steady drumbeat of neoconservative think-tank writers such as Chester Finn of the Thomas B. Fordham Institute (Broad Foundation & Thomas B. Fordham Institute, 2003) and Frederick Hess (2003) of the American Enterprise Institute, who have striven to deprofessionalize or remove leadership preparation from universities and reposition it in other social sites in the education field, or erase such preparation requirements altogether. This repositioning is part of a larger neoconservative strategy to marketize education (Anderson & Pini, 2011; Apple, 2006; Blackmore, 2013; English, 2014; Kumashiro, 2008).

The shift to the state level has become the battleground for all groups in vying for power and influence within the educational field—by those who want to enhance state power to regulate licensure practices more heavily and implement the Common Core curriculum standards and, paradoxically, by those neoconservatives who want to deregulate the very same practices by loosening state requirements or changing the manner of preparing school leaders required by the state to enable alternative places or practices and deprofessionalize leadership preparation.

The struggle is about dominance, and one can see the form that the conflict over influence has taken in the op-ed columns, the position papers of the neoconservative think tanks, the policies of the U.S. Department of Education, and the agendas of various state legislatures. The conflict over basic values has been cleanly sculpted out. The argument is centered on who shall lead the schools, based on what values, and for what social and educational ends. The outcome is usually a law, regulation, or policy, because in these forms the truly arbitrary nature of the decision is disguised "by dint of the fact that it can present itself under the appearances of universality—that of reason and morality" (Bourdieu, 1990b, p. 85). We will see how this has worked in the field of educational preparation.

Figure 4.1 illustrates the recent field of power in U.S. education at the national level. Unlike many other countries, there is no national ministry of education in America. Education has been centered in the 50 states individually, according to the provisions of the Tenth Amendment to the U.S. Constitution.

This has meant that with a historically weak (but growing) central body directing national education efforts, in the guise of the U.S. Department of Education, the matters of state governance, licensure of teachers and other educational officers, and regulation of preparation programs has devolved from essentially one agency—that is, the university followed by the department of education in each state—to many agencies. The agencies in the field are listed below:

American Association of School Administrators (AASA)

American Educational Research Association (AERA)

Association for Supervision and Curriculum Development (ASCD)

Council of Chief State School Officers (CCSSO)

Educational Leadership Constituent Council (ELCC)

Educational Testing Service (ETS)

Interstate School Leaders Licensure Assessment (ISLLA)

Interstate School Leaders Licensure Consortium (ISLLC)

National Association of Elementary School Principals (NAESP)

National Association of Secondary School Principals (NASSP)

National Council for the Accreditation of Teacher Education (NCATE)

National Council of Professors of Educational Administration (NCPEA)

National Policy Board for Educational Administration (NPBEA)

Teacher Education Accreditation Council (TEAC)

University Council for Educational Administration (UCEA)

The logic of the Bourdieusian educational field in the United States has been anchored in issues of preparation and licensure. Indeed, this grounding is one of the peculiar logics in Bourdieu's notion of the logic of practice. Those agencies and institutions that controlled these activities were the most powerful and influential. Later, when the logic of accreditation was installed as a form of inspection and policing, the policing agency was added to the logic of the field. In the United States, accreditation was carried out by the

Figure 4.1   The National Field for Educational Leadership in the United States

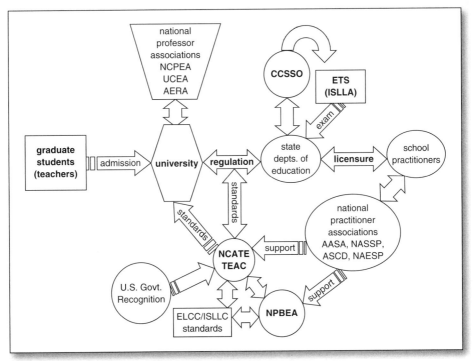

NCATE in conjunction with the respective state departments of education and other regional accreditation agencies.

What has changed within the past two decades has been the influence of the neoconservative foundations and think tanks (Bumiller, 2008; Maxwell, 2006; Sawchuk, 2012), which have mounted a concerted attack on the historic and long-standing agencies and institutions controlling preparation, licensure, and accreditation in the education field, as shown in Figure 4.2. The most recent move in this attack is a special report (Briggs, Cheney, Davis, & Moll, 2013) from the new neoconservative think tank in Dallas, Texas—the George W. Bush Institute—which is financed by historic right-wing funders.

These agencies and think tanks have elbowed their way into a position of influence with huge expenditures that establish programs, institutes, and alternative groups to support the commodification and privatization of the public education field (Dillon, 2011; Riley, 2011). The think tanks and foundations have actively supported politicians who favor their agendas, even influencing elections to local boards of education in urban centers and spending large sums to curb the power

Figure 4.2   The Assault by Neoliberal Think Tanks on the Educational Field

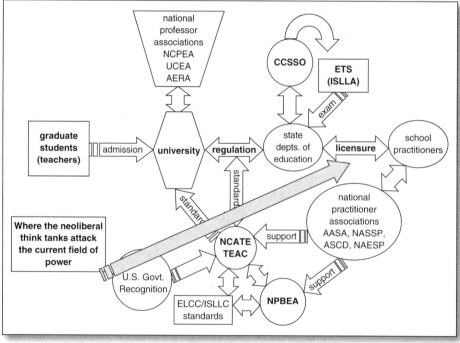

Reprinted with permission from the publisher, Proactive Publications.

of teachers unions at the local and state levels. Their influence has not gone without criticism (Ravitch, 2010a; Sawchuk, 2012), but it is also a testimony to Bourdieu's point that among the three forms of capital (economic, cultural, and social) economic capital (material wealth) is the most potent and immediate in producing an impact.

As a result of this two-decade assault, most recently seen in the George W. Bush Foundation's report attacking licensure practices by state departments of education (Briggs et al., 2013), the field of power has shifted. The influence of universities, along with that of professorial organizations, has declined. One outcome is that, for school administrators to occupy leadership positions, they can be alternatively certified directly by school districts and practitioner organizations or certification requirements can be waived. Administrators in many states are no longer exclusively prepared in university or college settings.

Figure 4.3 shows which agencies have gained power and influence—the NCATE, the CCSSO, and state departments of education. In the political sense, state legislatures have become more active in

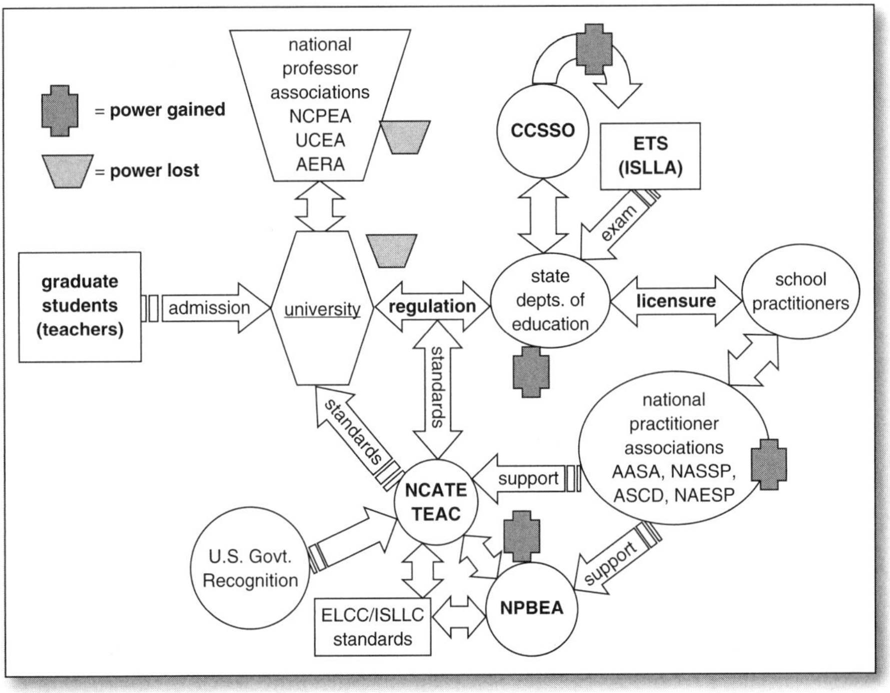

Figure 4.3 Changes in the Power and Influence of Agencies in the Educational Field

promoting neoliberal laws and regulations, and in the cities mayors have worked to wrest control of the schools from elected or appointed boards of education.

Under the neoconservative mantra of criticizing a monopoly, which hampers creativity and the creation of more efficient (cheaper) means, the logic of licensure has been systematically attacked (Hess, 2003).

Part of the rationale for this attack is the idea that leadership ability is essentially genetic and that licensure is therefore an artificial device that blocks the schools' capacity to attract "top talent" (Broad Foundation & Thomas B. Fordham Institute, 2003). Bourdieu and Passeron (1979) called this idea "charisma ideology," in which the privileges of the upper classes are recast as possessing "individual grace" (p. 70). Khurana (2002) expressed a similar idea when he indicated that in business organizations many members of boards of directors believe that "the charisma they seek in candidates [for CEO] is something that comes through inheritance and early formative experiences and cannot be learned or acquired later in life" (p. 153).

The result of the neoconservative assault has been the passage of legislation in many states that allows for licensure to be bestowed on individuals outside of the university, through direct acquisition by school districts and practitioner organizations, by creating localized "leadership academies" that teach aspiring school principals the "practical knowledge" they need to be successful in largely urban settings. If preparation for a profession is carried out on a university campus, such as in law and medical schools, then the neoliberal attack has deprofessionalized educational leadership. University curricula have been criticized by neoconservative critics such as Hess (2003) and later the George W. Bush Foundation (Briggs et al., 2013).

The neoconservative attack has been aimed at wresting control and influence from the university and schools of education, arguing that preparation practices are either too theoretical or too soft to take on the "hard" management issues confronting urban schools today (Hess & Kelly, 2005). The point is then made that such "hard" management matters are taught in schools of business and the military, and that forcing potential candidates to take classes in schools of education erects artificial barriers that keep talent out of school management (Broad Foundation & Thomas B. Fordham Institute, 2003).

The Broad Superintendents Academy is an attempt by billionaire Eli Broad to "open up" the ranks of potential leaders for urban schools—largely with political leaders, most but not all of whom are

Republicans—to support approaches that allow noneducators to assume educational leadership positions in such cities as Chicago, Los Angeles, New York, and New Orleans. To date, the records of noneducators leading such systems have been less than convincing and their terms of office about the same as those of educators (English & Crowder, 2013).

What is clear from the billionaires who have determined to change educational leadership through bypassing traditional channels of preparation and ignoring licensure issues is that the insertion of huge amounts of material capital can change the logic of a field and alter the respective power and influence of actors and agencies already in that field. The influence of universities and professors in the field has steadily shrunk, to the point that they have become simply the means to implement state initiatives centered on neoconservative initiatives and the commodification of schools to be privatized and run by pro-profit individuals and private educational management organizations (Anderson & Pini, 2011; English, 2014).

One agency that has gained influence in the educational field is the U.S. Department of Education, with billions of dollars in the so-called Race to the Top initiative, based on standardized test scores and linking teacher and principal pay to gains on these scores, breaking the power of teachers unions, and pushing new ways to "evaluate" teachers on their performance. So the power of teachers unions has also diminished in the churning of the field.

The influence of state departments of education has increased with the emphasis on the Common Core curriculum standards but diminished in their sole power to license teachers and school administrators. The power of schools of education has also been diminished, where routes to the teaching profession are more and more being taken outside of their jurisdiction and control, and other options, such as Teach for America, are growing in their efforts to shorten the preparation period for teachers and place them in urban and rural school settings.

Despite the fact that the records of the alternatively certified teachers are worse than those of teachers who have been conventionally trained, Teach for America remains popular because it is a cheaper form of preparation and also conforms to the idea that anyone who "knows" how to do something can teach it to others, ignoring abundant evidence to the contrary (see Aronson, 2013).

U.S. schools of education have been contested places wherein are found liberal ideas regarding teacher empowerment and democratic education ideas that challenge conventional notions of hierarchy and control, much to the chagrin of neoliberal pundits such as Finn (1991), as expressed in his book *We Must Take Charge*.

The notion of contestation in the Bourdieusian field is amply evidenced in the United States, especially in the form of economic capital, and is illustrative of how much influence can be acquired by those who are willing to spend economic capital in a sustained manner in highly selective settings (Davis, 2013). The political discourse has changed. The political right has been extremely successful in framing the educational debate (Kumashiro, 2008). The vocabulary and diagnosis of what's wrong with the schools has become a "common-sense" perspective, echoed in the editorial pages of *The Wall Street Journal, USA Today, Los Angeles Times,* and many other media outlets, with common-sense antidotes for the nation's "failing schools" not far behind (Emery & Ohanian, 2004). The neoconservative ideology has been disguised and passed off as "disinterested" recommendation.

A HARD LOOK BACK: A TRAJECTORY OF CLASS CONTROL OF SCHOOLS AND EDUCATION

We have already commented on the fact that, from its inception in America, public education has favored the higher social classes (Katz, 1968). It is similarly the fate of the ISLLC standards that in their embodiment as a "core technology" they, too, fail to address the significant socioeconomic disparities and inequities that exist in the larger society and instead focus only on internal means to raise achievement. Thus, they contribute to the continuing reproduction of socioeconomic inequalities in American life.

The ISLLC standards, by ignoring the larger role of schools in U.S. society as legitimizing agents of socioeconomic disparities, perpetuate the very inequities they were designed to ameliorate by simply ignoring them. And, while *social justice* is finally included in the latest revision of the ISLLC standards, it is not defined and is confined to ensuring "that student needs inform all aspects of schooling" (CCSSO, 2008, p. 15). Since schools are reproductive and legitimizing agents of the larger social hierarchies in place, this statement about social justice does not address the real cause of social injustice or the school's role in legitimizing it.

Following conceptual Step 1, Steps 2 and 3 in the United States saw the "core technology" become the "knowledge base"—that is, a political platform on which to erect the licensure and testing requirements needed to affirm or deny that a candidate for school leadership possesses the designated leadership competencies. The entire enterprise assumes a permanency and stability politically required for bureaucratic rationality to become operational (Bottery, 2004), and the mummified role is then subdivided into realms, themes, and performance-level indicators. Conceptual Step 4 involved "validating the list of competencies via professional consensus by surveying practitioners to determine if they believed such indicators were accurate descriptors of their actual duties as principals" (Educational Testing Service, 1997). However, as English (2000) observed, "polling practitioners regarding best practice amounts to an epistemology which asserts that knowing and doing constitute truth" (p. 160), something Lakatos (1999, p. 35) describes as a descendant of divine revelation.

A Bourdieusian frame offers a poignant example of how actor-agents within a contested field—in this case, professors and practitioners—vie for positions of power and dominance, and how it remains so to this day. Originally, the impetus for national standards in the United States emanated from institutions of higher education. Martha McCarthy (1999) recounted that the UCEA established the National Commission on Excellence in Educational Administration (NCEEA) in 1985. In a document titled *Leaders for America's Schools*, released 2 years later, an observation was made "that at least 300 of the 500 institutions offering courses in educational administration should eliminate such offerings because their programs were inadequate" (Griffiths, Stout, & Forsyth, 1988, p. 20).

Under the guise of upgrading preparation, this move, what Bourdieu would call a "pedagogic action," extended the power and reach of those proffering it, simultaneously wrapped within the content of the action that legitimized it and the power to proclaim it. This duality is part of the process of concealment based on misrecognition of an essentially arbitrary action. The concealment also shields the action from questions pertaining to the bestowal of legitimacy to engage in it at all. In the case of the NCEEA, nobody apparently asked, "Who gave this group the authority and legitimacy to engage in such a study and issue a report in the first place?"

The political purpose of the NCEEA in the professional field was to put out of business some institutions that prepared educational leaders. Unfortunately, it backfired when the national leadership practitioner associations became involved. Those associations of principals and superintendents became key political players. With this involvement, the power within the field shifted rather dramatically. Perhaps the most prominent player was the CCSSO, within which the ISLLC, represented by 24 state departments of education and 11 national school leader (practitioner) associations (Shipman et al., 2007), was established in 1994.

This shift took the focus off issues of leadership preparation, as well as larger epistemological issues, centered in the university setting and placed it on behavioral skill sets embedded in a market-oriented neoliberal perspective (Murphy, 1999). Another group within this movement was the ELCC, which came to oversee professional accreditation of university/college programs under the auspices of the NPBEA and NCATE. Practitioner associations have played a key funding and sponsorship role, and the ISLLC standards themselves are the property of the CCSSO. This difference between the United States and England makes the prospect of resistance to the standards very remote in the former, but Thomson (2008) considered headship association resistance to performativity standards to be a possibility in England.

There were grandiose and sweeping objectives for the ISLLC standards in the United States. According to Murphy (2005), the aim of the ISLLC was "to create a set of standards that would provide the basis for reshaping the profession of school administration in the United States" and "to direct action in the academic, policy, and practice domains of the profession consistent with those perspectives across an array of strategy leverage points (e.g., licensure, professional development, administrator evaluation" (p. 155). The ISLLC itself, as its first director explained, was "created by those most knowledgeable and in control of the field of educational administration in the United States at the time" (Shipman, 2006, pp. 524–526).

The effect of the continuing rise of the standards movement has been to create political hegemony over an entire field and, most tragically, to cast a pall over other forms of inquiry not viewed as important or relevant that would challenge the efficacy of the standards themselves. For example, a report by Schneider and Fede (2002) to the NPBEA noted that 75% of the "denied" departments of educational administration for accreditation required courses in foundations (meaning history and philosophy), compared with only 25% of the "nationally recognized departments" (p. 11).

This judgment matches Bourdieu's (1991) observation that

> the political field in fact produces an effect of censorship by limiting the universe of political discourse, and thus what is politically thinkable, to the finite space of discourses capable of being produced or reproduced within the limits of the political problematic ... the boundary between what is politically sayable or unsayable, thinkable or unthinkable. (p. 172)

THE DECONTEXTUALIZATION OF SCHOOL LEADERS VIA JOB STANDARDIZATION

To understand why the ISLLC standards won't change anything in school leadership, it is necessary to retrace their creation. In the standards, the decision that "there is a single set of standards that applies to all leadership positions" is simply stated as a "tenet"—that is, an article of faith (Murphy et al., 2000, p. 23). In this move, job contextuality is removed and a "one-size-fits-all" description is developed. In this construction, important differences between roles are erased or marginalized. In other cases, some skills desirable and necessary at one level may be unnecessary or performed very differently at the next level, so reductionism is occurring. Complex roles are deskilled and dumbed down.

For example, an indicator of ISLLC Standard 4 is to "build and sustain positive relationships with families and caregivers" as a way of assessing whether an education leader is "collaborating with faculty and community members, responding to diverse community interests and needs, and mobilizing community resources" (CCSSO, 2008, p. 15). This indicator would apply to the school-site level rather directly but in quite a different manner for a U.S. superintendent of schools. An important factor in the job performance of a superintendent of schools is to work effectively with an elected or appointed board of education. There is no ISLLC standard or indicator that touches on this aspect of a superintendent's job in the United States. In addition, in states where collective bargaining is practiced, there is no ISLLC standard or indicator involving this critical component of district-level management.

This is curious because the construction of the "core technology" is a way to buffer internal functions against meddling. A contract with the teachers union most assuredly touches on many aspects of teaching, such as the length of the workday, preparation, staff development, evaluation, work innovation, and many other factors on which hinge day-to-day teaching practices. However, this feature is absent from the standards as an important job skill. Standardization has removed both role specificity and contextuality in performing this aspect of the superintendent's responsibilities.

A simple retracing of these steps indicates that if one freezes a single role within a field and that role is connected to all other roles within a hierarchy, then the relationships are similarly frozen—that is, reified. And if all the roles are embedded within a constellation whose axes are about social conservatism, then creating lists of skills amounts to a form of social mummification and becomes itself a formidable barrier to change, because a change agent would have to unpack the entire field to establish a new center of gravity.

The final irony of the reification of the status quo in the creation of national standards for educational leaders is that these standards will continue to cast school leaders in the role of agents of social inequality, and that will not reform anything. This situation occurs when a truncated, miniaturized, static knowledge base is imposed on graduate-level training to produce "new leaders" but these leaders have been prepared in a frozen relationship with other roles in the hierarchy within a field and with the same old skill sets lodged in the current logic of practice. Codification of leaders via standardization is not innovation and promises no reform; rather, it is a kind of scholasticism (English & Papa, 2010).

Because the standards are lodged and validated in the doxa of the times, they will remain viable only if schools and the larger socioeconomic social space in which they remain also stay fixed. They will not challenge the conservative political ideology and social inequalities that are at the root of the achievement gap. The possibility that they will offer any promise of substantive change is mythological. Groopman (2010) calls this an example of a "focusing illusion," which "occurs when, basing our predictions on a single change in the status quo, we mistakenly forecast dramatic effects on an overall condition" (pp. 12–15). He similarly warns that in medicine "past efforts to standardize and broadly mandate *best practices* were scientifically misconceived" (Groopman, 2007, p. 11). This happens when a set of practices is believed to be independent of the patients' responses. But in schools, as in medicine, so-called "best practices" in many cases are *interactive* and *interdependent* with those responses. To believe that the ISLLC standards are good for all leaders in all situations at all times is an example of a focusing illusion—that is, misrecognition.

THE REFORMERS' BLINKERED VISION
FOR CHANGE: THEY JUST DON'T SEE IT

While the rhetoric of proponents of the ISLLC standards promises "transformation" and "reculturing," the reality is that they will simply produce the "same old, same old." The proponents are neither objective nor privileged except by their own claims, and schools under this imprimatur of leadership will continue to do what they have always done: reproduce the status quo—inequities, achievement gaps, and all.

The continuing governmental coercion to replicate leaders according to such standards will lead to an expensive and bitter disappointment. However, as these agents and agencies fail to understand their own misrecognition, the very leaders mass-produced in preparation programs, as well as the preparation programs themselves, will once again be blamed.

The irony of standardizing one's way to excellence acting as a barrier to excellence itself also goes unrecognized. The reason is not hard to discern, for, as LiPuma (1993) noted, "the symbolic order 'owes its structure' to the social conditions of its production and circulation, and its particular 'force' to the fact that the power relations which it expresses are manifest 'in the misrecognizable form of relations of meaning'" (p. 20). The connection between the power to impose the standards and the standards that contain the power to exercise that control cannot be deconstructed by the proponents. They just don't get it.

IMPLICATIONS FOR POLICY AND PRACTICE

Ideologies and the Interrelational World of Educational Policy and Practice

1. At this juncture, the reader should be seeing that Bourdieu's sociological world was interactive and dynamic even as the forces in that world worked hard to maintain their positions of dominance in their respective fields. The importance of language as both a symbol of attempts to influence and expand agents and/or agencies within a field and a symbol to impose a particular manner of thinking and viewing things works powerfully in education as in every other field. Boudon (1989) explains that an ideology consists of "those abstract (and rather dubious) theories allegedly based on reason or science, which tried to map out the social order and guide political action" (p. 25).

   Current ideologies are largely concerned with matters of so-called "reform" and accountability masked in a variety of terms in which the ideologies (as political narratives) are rarely if ever deconstructed to reveal they often negate that which they proclaim to advance.

2. There are no neutral combatants in Bourdieu's world. He sees confrontation and contestation as inevitable and never ending, because "legitimacy is indivisible: there is no agency to

legitimate the legitimacy-giving agencies, because claims to legitimacy derive their relative strength, in the last analysis, from the strength of the groups or classes whose material and symbolic interests they directly or indirectly express" (Bourdieu & Passeron, 1970/2000, p. 18).

Educators, teachers, and school leaders should begin to see the larger socioeconomic political world with new eyes. Reformers advance their positions for change, often hiding their own self-interests or stakes embedded in the changes they advocate. A useful tactic is to ask, "Who benefits and who doesn't benefit from what is being proposed?"

Educational Leadership Preparation Remains in a Confused and Contested State

Neoconservative ideas and forces have exerted enormous influence on the nature of leadership preparation. In the United Kingdom, neoconservative policies of the former Tony Blair ministry removed the necessity of a university master's degree and preparation from the process to become a head teacher; instead, all that is required is professional development courses from the National College for School Leadership. This move effectively nullified legitimate consideration of alternative perspectives regarding the nature of school leadership.

In the United States, leadership preparation is still governed by the requirements of the 50 states but is increasingly becoming nationalized via accreditation and state legislative agendas shaped by conservative politicians. Increasingly, the framework and content of school leadership are being recast along the lines of envisioning the work as commodification of formerly public space in the guise of "choice," with voucher plans and charter schools in the forefront. This approach appeals to the public under the mantra of "the freedom to choose."

The emerging evidence shows that charter schools are no more effective than regular public schools and that they do not speed up the process of reform or innovation as their advocates often claim (see English, 2014). The opening up of formerly public space to privatization has created new markets for those desiring to make money selling their wares. It has also relieved the drive to improve public education with increased funding, since the failure of the schools to educate the poor is not because there are no good schools open to them but because parents make poor choices among the schools available. Once again, the victims are blamed for their own plight.

The Battle for the Dominant Ideology of School Leadership Continues

Policy developers who believe schools can be improved with more general competition for the scarce resources allocated to education embrace a "for-profit" mind-set regarding school leadership. Schools must be marketed and "sold" to the public, who are looking for a commodity to advantage their children. This mind-set ignores the growing inequalities between the haves and have-nots in the United Kingdom and the United States, which are among the largest of modern countries in the world and becoming larger, to the point that President Barack Obama has made "a dangerous and growing inequality and lack of upward mobility the defining challenge of our time" (Grady, 2013, p. A15).

Very few of the educational reformers in either the United Kingdom or the United States have made the growing gap between various social classes a prominent objective for their educational systems. Social justice issues have been pushed to the back burner, if they are considered at all. Instead, the litany of goals for national educational reforms is about creating and maintaining national competitiveness in the world of commerce and business. The agenda of economic domination sees the schools of each of our nations as the means toward those ends. Education is not good as a means of becoming more human and humane; rather, education is about maintaining the division of wealth available to be acquired within the concept of globalization and ensuring that most of it, or as much as possible, is garnered by each country respectively.

Within this concept of global competitiveness, the schools are the instruments of attaining the primacy sought. The role of the school leader becomes that of ensuring this quest by the cheapest possible means. Each nation has adopted policies that amount to a new form of monopoly even as they parade their changes under the guise of promoting diversity. That monopoly begins with an epistemology centered on the logic of the marketplace as the ultimate determiner of what is a "good education."

KEY CHAPTER CONCEPTS

field of power

Wacquant (1992) indicates that the *field of power* should be thought of as a kind of "meta-field" (p. 18). Each field is unique and possesses its own logic. This logic is revealed by mapping out the objective structure of the agents in a particular field and trying to understand how they compete for specific forms of influence and authority. This method involves analyzing the habitus of the agents in the fields and how their systems of dispositions determine who they are and what kinds of roles they may play in any of the choices involved.

Thomson (2009) similarly described the Bourdieusian perspective: "There is no level playing ground in a social field; players who begin with particular forms of capital are advantaged at the outset because the field depends on, as well as produces more of, that capital" (p. 69). Each field functions semiautonomously and has its own set of beliefs (or theodicies) that form a logic of practice.

Bourdieu (1996) provided a more familiar metaphor of the dual aspects of a field of power by comparing a field to an old house in which many occupants have lived. While all the occupants have made changes in the house, they have had to conform to some of the choices made by previous inhabitants within the house's structure. This structure acts as a barrier to change, and when occupants come to accept the structure, they are products of it and are shaped by it. As individual occupants work within the structure, they also perpetuate it. The house is thus a "structuring structure," in that it is both passive (it exists as it is and has an objective presence) and active (it shapes the perceptions of and imposes its limitations on the inhabitants) because it is part and parcel of habitus.

The field of power is thus one of Bourdieu's most interrelational and fluid ideas. It is simultaneously liberating and limiting. In the case of the development of leadership standards in the United Kingdom and the United States, the language of the standards seems to be about optimizing the strengths of individual schools, but in reality it is about making all the schools the same (English, 2003).

managerialism

This is an approach to leading organizations or agencies based on the principles of Frederick Taylor (1856–1915). In *managerialism* (earlier called Taylorism), the preoccupation of management is control of the worker and the rigid subdivision of the work into smaller tasks to reduce the costs of high-priced labor and permit application of rigid cost controls and profit maximization (see Kanigel, 1997). Most of the popular accountability approaches in education are based on the principles of managerialism. The preoccupation with controlling the work usually leads to an approach of top-down authoritarian management and confrontation with labor unions over work rules and tenure.

5

A Retrospective Look at Bourdieu's Impact

❖ ❖ ❖

WHAT THIS CHAPTER IS ABOUT

Pierre Bourdieu's relevance to educational issues today has never been more crucial. While he served on some commissions in France that dealt with education, his academic credentials and his stature were never those of a reformer. The basis of his work was about inequality and the failure of the French state to deal with those issues of which education was but one critical function. He was a tireless advocate for **social justice** issues, a public intellectual, and a militant combatant against the forces of **neoliberalism** (sometimes called neo-conservatism) that were heavily impacting France at the time of his death in 2002.

In this chapter, we review what we believe to be Bourdieu's most important thoughts and work in education from the perspective of practitioners and policymakers who are engaged in a similar struggle. The rhetoric of reform is everywhere, but as Bourdieu so presciently pointed out, neoliberal notions of reform are really a throwback to a much earlier form of capitalism in which the gains for the care of the poor and the minimal guarantees of a decent life for all people from the state have become the targets of derision and erasure. Bourdieu's "left hand" and "right hand" metaphor of the state captures this conflict very well. The left hand represents programs of social welfare and education. The right hand represents programs of business and commerce.

Since Bourdieu did not write directly about many practical educational issues, we base our judgments regarding what he might say about contemporary educational ideas some 11 years after his death on the corpus of his published writing in English, some selected scholarly opinions about his various positions, and what we believe to be logical extensions based on his lines of argument as we understand them.

Specifically, this chapter addresses the following points:

- Some of the main points of Bourdieu's work will help educators and policy developers more clearly understand why past educational reforms did not work and why.

- A move toward enlarging the success rate for all students begins with those who are not well served by the schools as they currently exist.

INTRODUCTION

Bourdieu's work, as discussed previously, was centered on the dynamics of power in social fields, the interaction of habitus and capital, together with the structure and interrelationships within them. Education was one field in which Bourdieu and his colleagues wrote a great deal (Bourdieu, 1984/2009, 1996; Bourdieu & Passeron, 1970/2000, 1979). Bourdieu's elevation of cultural and social capital that were eventually transferred to economic capital was one of his important contributions to an understanding of how power and wealth interacted to produce influence within social fields.

THE SOCIAL FIELD OF EDUCATION IS NOT STATIC

Bourdieu's conceptualization of a field as a site of actors and agencies engaged in a struggle for legitimacy and influence is surely reflective of education today in the United Kingdom, United States, and other countries. The fact that they are hierarchically arranged is also apparent. Some have attained greater positions of influence than others—for example, the high number of former Eli Broad and Bill Gates employees and acolytes who have found positions in the

Barack Obama administration's Department of Education under the leadership of Arne Duncan, a noneducator who has advanced a broad, top-down neoconservative agenda heavily laced with managerialist trappings.

Bourdieu's observation that conflict and contestation are inevitable and continuous because there is no final arbiter regarding legitimacy underscores the importance of establishing political coalitions. It also emphasizes why the cause of public education and social justice must be fought in each generation. There will never be a time when schools are not caught up in various forms of political struggle. School agents must be active politically in this contest. To take oneself out of this conflict is to let others determine one's fate. The perspective that schools must be "above" politics is not only a myth but a huge handicap in opposing the forces of neoconservatism that are actively working to deprofessionalize and privatize public education.

School leaders, teachers, and parents need to understand that unless they are able to forge relationships with other actors and agencies in this contested social field, their influence will be confined and limited by the acquisition of the forms of capital within their reach. The most influential form of capital is economic, and here the "billionaire boys club" provides an illustration of the centrality of economic capital, as this group is able to exercise distinct advantages in the United States (Ravitch, 2010a).

EDUCATION IS SIMULTANEOUSLY A MEANS AND AN END

Education is a means to acquire more symbolic capital and, ultimately, more economic capital in the marketplace. Education is also an end in that it is not a socially neutral institution and comprises methods, procedures, and curriculum content that are closely aligned with the interests of the agents who control it. Control exists on multiple fronts. School-based procedures parallel those of a particular social group. The curriculum content of a school is that which is believed by the same social agents to be "best" for them and "best" for everyone. Education is thus a form of cultural, economic, and social reproduction. Education controlled by the state constitutes a form of social legitimacy. It cloaks the interests of those who are in control in the guise of neutrality and portrays those interests as universal. Even those who find the values, methods, and content of schooling alien to themselves believe that their failure to do well is their fault and not that of the system. Bourdieu believed that the oppressed participate in their own oppression.

This is a hard position for those who are not doing well in the current system of schooling to understand. There is a tendency to want to amend or tinker with the system. Such things as culturally relevant teaching are proffered as a means to make the current system of schooling more acceptable and to improve the success of those children who represent a different cultural outlook and background in the schools. But this is only a Band-Aid for the issue. While culturally relevant teaching is better than a purely monocultural curriculum and the methods congruent with such a curriculum, the problem for those in schools is how to expand and make the process of schooling more inclusive of and relevant for all children.

SCHOOLING AS THE CULTURAL ARBITRARY DEMONIZES THOSE WHO ARE "OTHERIZED"

Bourdieu and his colleagues spoke of education and its content as the "cultural arbitrary" because schooling and its content are just one of many possible human constructs. The selection of one of those possibilities is congruent with the interests of those who are dominant within the social field. Those who find the cultural arbitrary difficult or foreign are often marginalized as less capable intellectually and culturally. In other words, they are "otherized" as "those people" who don't or can't see the many benefits the cultural arbitrary would bring to their lives. This enables those in control to blame those who are unsuccessful in the system for their own problems and shortcomings. This shift enables the system to continue without substantive change, even as it is clearly failing many of the children within it.

The recent push for the Common Core curriculum standards in the United States is just the latest example of a cultural arbitrary being promoted as something that is "good for all." It has been cloaked in endorsements from a bevy of public and private interest groups, from the U.S. Chamber of Commerce to state governor associations and the U.S. Department of Education. Despite these endorsements, the Common Core curriculum standards are not "common" to all groups or all students who attend public schools. They are an example of a monocultural curriculum being passed off as universal. As such, they will not resolve the achievement gap but are likely only to perpetuate and extend it. This question should be asked: "To whom is this curriculum common?"

THE DOMINANT CONSUMER CULTURE IN EDUCATION UNDERMINES ITS MORAL AND HUMANISTIC VALUE

The continued emphasis on education as primarily a means to get a job undermines the moral and humanistic purpose of education, which is to enable children to become more fully human. Harping on the value of education as solely determined by the existing jobs in the marketplace ties schooling to the perpetuation of the industrial/technological status quo. Many jobs today will not be jobs tomorrow. The sole emphasis on economic wealth as tied to the workplace creates a value orientation defined exclusively by the acquisition of a credential, as opposed to the broadening potential of a holistic education centered on good work habits or on the discipline through which intellectual growth occurs. To frame education as simply a process of acquiring credentials encourages students to slide through school with minimum effort and at the end expect their credentials to provide a cozy existence.

Bourdieu fought valiantly against the marketization of education and other social functions in France. In this concern, he showed prescience.

EDUCATIONAL REFORM WILL ALWAYS BENEFIT AND ADVANTAGE THE REFORMERS

Given the view that schooling benefits those whose home and social interests are most similar to those found in schools, most so-called reforms will be the ones that continue to advantage those already advantaged. There is nothing democratic about this process. Curriculum content is not voted on by all the people; rather, it has always been created through an elaborate social sorting process in which reforms are approved by elite groups that ostensibly have the expert credentials to select the "best" or "most appropriate" content (see McDonnell & Weatherford, 2013).

School reform works to the advantage of the reformers. They and/or the groups they represent stand to retain the advantages they hold in the educational system as it is. Bourdieu's work clearly shows that those working to change the system rarely, if ever, alter the schooling process to place themselves at a disadvantage. Reforms are never neutral.

THE DILEMMA OF SCHOOL LEADERSHIP: AGENT OF THE STATE OR OF HUMANITY?

Since licensure is the province of the state and the state's interests are not to benefit all students equally, the dilemma for school leadership is this: How should school leaders step out of the orthodoxy of the state and serve a broader purpose? If the state's primary interest in schooling is to provide skills for employment via school learning and present curricula that advance the interests of those who are already advantaged, how can school leaders strive for anything different? What are the risks in opposing the processes of the state, especially when new state laws give the state power to evaluate leaders and teachers based on standardized test scores and then fire underperforming educators? Bourdieu's work underscores how the interests of the dominant social and class groups work to perpetuate their advantages with the schooling process. The apparatus of the state is clearly aligned with those dominant interests.

There are few nations where leaders in public education can call into question the dominant and ruling interests of the government that licenses them to work as school leaders. While, in theory, separating schools into private spheres might encourage such deviations from the prevailing orthodoxies, the reality is that almost no nations do that. Privatizing education has not served to innovate or move schooling in broad new directions. It has, rather, simply created new markets for vendors to make money with new buyers.

IMPLICATIONS FOR POLICY AND PRACTICE

Can the Logic of Practice Be Changed?

At first blush, Bourdieu's work paints a fairly bleak picture of a schooling process deeply biased and highly resistant to substantive change. We do not find his work so pessimistic. We think of the billions of dollars and pounds spent on trying to reform schools with very few results to show for it over time. The schools keep working as they have always worked. The same students who have always done well continue to do well. And students from the working classes continue to see rather meager results from their efforts. Bourdieu's work helps us understand why this is so and why it will continue to be so until we recognize how schools can actually be changed.

To change schools so they are more successful with a wider band of students will require that those in the dominant groups and classes recognize and accept that their "cultural arbitrary" is simply one of many possibilities for schools to embrace. This is no easy feat. For example, definitions of academic success will have to become more broadly defined and more culturally inclusive, with wider bands of acceptable curricula than those currently embraced.

The so-called reforms of today are in reality a thin slice of rigid standardization, a one-size-fits-all curriculum, and a classic Procrustean bed of methods and procedures that are deeply alienating to some groups of students, many of whom drop out or are forced out of schools because they don't fit in.

If there is a bottom line, it is this: The continuing gap of wealth in the United Kingdom and the United States threatens the future of democracy in both countries. Schools serve to reinforce and reproduce that wealth gap. This predicament explains the position of Bourdieu and others pertaining to the concept of social justice. But little will be changed until and unless those with the social power to effect change recognize that it is in their own best interest to do so. In short, what is required is a "new gaze," a kind of metanoia, a new way of visualizing phenomena in the social world (Bolton, 2011).

Bourdieu's work helps us see what is at the center of this struggle. As he explained:

> Truth is the stake in a series of struggles in every field. The scientific field, which has reached a high degree of autonomy, has this peculiarity: you have a chance of success in it only if you conform to the immanent laws of the field, that is, if you recognize truth practically as a *value* and respect the methodological principles and canons defining *rationality* at the moment under consideration, at the same time as bringing into battle in the competitive struggles all the specific instruments that have been accumulated in the course of prior struggles. (Bourdieu, 1990b, p. 32)

This book has been about discerning the truth to sketch out a new vision. We cannot create a true metanoia without basing it on what actually exists and how the social and economic systems in which we live limit our choices by eliminating some of them at the outset. We are iteful to Bourdieu for helping us understand the basis for creating a better future for our children and our schools.

KEY CHAPTER CONCEPTS

neoliberalism

Sometimes referred to as neoconservatism, *neoliberalism* is a "theory of political economic practices that proposes that human well-being can best be advanced by liberating individual entrepreneurial freedoms and skills within an institutional framework characterized by strong private property rights, free markets, and free trade" (Harvey, 2005, p. 2). Neoliberal ideology holds that public education is a protected monopoly and therefore restricts the consumer from obtaining the best price and services. The solution is the marketization of public education and all social services to incentivize agencies within a specific sector to offer better services at lower costs. That services and expectations are similarly lowered is explained by indicating that over time the market will "take care of" such transgressions and drive those offering them out of business. The ideology of neoliberalism is advanced by appealing to the freedom to choose and the logic of greed (see English, 2014).

social justice

The concept of *social justice* is based on what constitutes "fairness" in a "good society" (Blackmore, 2013, p. 1001). At the center of the notion of social justice is the role of the state in ensuring that a society is just and fair and that inequalities based on race, gender, age, religion, and sexual orientation are absent from the distribution of wealth and social privileges in that society. The tenets of social justice stand in contradiction to the proponents of neoliberalism, because Bourdieu has shown that those who dominate social fields are those with the largest acquisition of the three forms of capital and they use the schools to legitimate and perpetuate their social dominance.

References

Alinsky, S. (1971). *Rules for radicals: A pragmatic primer for realistic radicals*. New York, NY: Vintage Books.

Anand, G. (2011, June 4). Class struggle: India's experiment in schooling tests rich and poor. *Wall Street Journal*, pp. A1, A10.

Anderson, G., & Pini, M. (2011). Educational leadership and the new economy: Keeping the "public" in the public schools. In F. English (Ed.), *The SAGE handbook of educational leadership* (2nd ed., pp. 176–222). Thousand Oaks, CA: SAGE.

Apple, M. (2004). Making white right: Race and the politics of educational reform. In M. Fine, L. Weis, L. Pruitt, & A. Burns (Eds.), *Off white: Readings on power, privilege, and resistance* (2nd ed., pp. 74–88). New York, NY: Routledge.

Apple, M. (2006). *Educating the "right" way: Markets, standards, God, and inequality* (2nd ed.). New York, NY: Routledge.

Archer, L., DeWitt, J., Osborne, J., Dillon, J., Willis, B., & Wong, B. (2012, October). Science aspirations, capital, and family habitus: How families shape children's engagement and identification with science. *American Educational Research Journal, 49*(5), 881–908.

Aronson, L. B. (2013, April 24). Advice to TFA from a former insider. *Education Week, 32*(29), 24.

Aschbacher, P. R., Li, E., & Roth, E. J. (2010). Is science me? High school students' identities, participation, and aspirations in science, engineering, and medicine. *Journal of Research in Science Teaching, 47*, 564–582.

Baker, D. P., Goesling, B., & Letendre, G. K. (2002). Socioeconomic status, school quality, and national economic development: A cross-national analysis of the Heyneman-Loxley effect. *Comparative Education Review, 46*(3), 291–312.

Banchero, S. (2011, January 6). Students score poorly on science test. *Wall Street Journal*, p. A2.

Barry, B. (2005). *Why social justice matters*. Cambridge, UK: Polity Press.

Bates, S. (1993). *Battleground*. New York, NY: Poseidon Press.

Berger, J. (1972). *Ways of seeing*. London: Penguin Books and the BBC.

Blackmore, J. (2013). Social justice in education: A theoretical overview.

In B. Irby, G. Brown, R. Lara-Alecio, & S. Jackson (Eds.), *The handbook of educational theories* (pp. 1001–1009). Charlotte, NC: Information Age.

Blau, P., & Scott, W. (1962). *Formal organizations*. San Francisco, CA: Chandler.

Board of Education of Oklahoma City v. Dowell, 498 U.S. 237 (1991).

Bolton, C. L. (2011). Metanoia in educational leadership: An alternative perspective for school leadership. In F. W. English (Ed.), *The SAGE handbook of educational leadership* (2nd ed., pp. 223–229). Thousand Oaks, CA: SAGE.

Bolton, C. L. (2013). *Investigating the professionalization of the English further education (FE) teacher workforce: A Bourdieusian analysis*. Unpublished doctoral dissertation, Staffordshire University, United Kingdom.

Bottery, M. (2004). *The challenges of educational leadership*. London: Paul Chapman.

Boudon, R. (1989). *The analysis of ideology* (M. Slater, Trans.). Chicago, IL: University of Chicago Press.

Bourdieu, P. (1971). Intellectual field and creative project. In M. F. D. Young (Ed.), *Knowledge and control: New directions for the sociology of education* (pp. 161–188). London: Collier-Macmillan.

Bourdieu, P. (1977). *Outline of a theory of practice* (R. Nice, Trans.). Cambridge, UK: Cambridge University Press. (Original work published in 1972)

Bourdieu, P. (1984). *Distinction: A social critique of the judgment of taste* (R. Nice, Trans.). Cambridge, MA: Harvard University Press.

Bourdieu, P. (1986). The forms of capital (R. Nice, Trans.). In J. Richardson (Ed.), *Handbook of theory and research for the sociology of education* (pp. 241–258). New York, NY: Greenwood Press.

Bourdieu, P. (1989a). *Distinction: A social critique of the judgment of taste* (R. Nice, Trans.). Oxford, UK: Taylor & Francis.

Bourdieu, P. (1989b). *La Noblesse d'etat: Grands corps et grandes ecoles*. Paris: Editions de Minuit.

Bourdieu, P. (1990a). *The logic of practice*. Cambridge, UK: Polity Press. (Original work published in 1980)

Bourdieu, P. (1990b). *In other words: Essays towards a reflexive sociology*. Stanford, CA: Stanford University Press.

Bourdieu, P. (1991). *Language and symbolic power*. Cambridge, MA: Harvard University Press.

Bourdieu, P. (1992). *The rules of art: Genesis and structure of the literary field*. Stanford, CA: Stanford University Press.

Bourdieu, P. (1993). *The field of cultural production*. New York, NY: Columbia University Press.

Bourdieu, P. (1996). *The state nobility: Elite schools in the field of power* (L. C. Clough, Trans.). Stanford, CA: Stanford University Press.

Bourdieu, P. (1998). *Practical reason: On the theory of action*. Stanford, CA: Stanford University Press.

Bourdieu, P. (1999). Site effects. In P. Bourdieu et al. (Eds.), *The weight of the world: Social suffering in contemporary society* (pp. 123–129). Stanford, CA: Stanford University Press.

Bourdieu, P. (2000). *Pascalian meditations* (R. Nice, Trans.). Cambridge, UK: Polity.

Bourdieu, P. (2001). *Masculine domination* (R. Nice, Trans.). Stanford, CA: Stanford University Press.

Bourdieu, P. (2004a). *Science of science and reflexivity* (R. Nice, Trans.). Chicago, IL: University of Chicago Press.

Bourdieu, P. (2004b). *Sketch for a self-analysis*. Chicago, IL: University of Chicago Press.

Bourdieu, P. (2008). A look back at the reception of *The Inheritors* and *Reproduction in Education*. In F. Poupeau & T. Discepolo (Eds.), *Political interventions: Social science and political action* (D. Fernbach, Trans., pp. 49–53). London: Verso.

Bourdieu, P. (2009). *Distinction: A social critique of the judgment of taste* (R. Nice, Trans.). New York, NY: Routledge. (Original work published in 1984)

Bourdieu, P., & Passeron, J.-C. (1979). *The inheritors*. Chicago, IL: University of Chicago Press.

Bourdieu, P., & Passeron, J.-C. (2000). *Reproduction in education, society and culture* (2nd ed., R. Nice, Trans.). London: SAGE. (Original work published in 1970)

Bourdieu, P., & Wacquant, L. J. D. (1992). *An invitation to reflexive sociology*. Chicago, IL: University of Chicago Press.

Bowles, S., & Gintis, H. (1976). *Schooling in capitalist America: Educational reform and the contradictions of economic life*. New York, NY: Basic Books.

Boykin, A. (1986). The triple quandary and the schooling of Afro-American children. In U. Neisser (Ed.), *The school achievement of minority children: New perspectives*

(pp. 57–92). Hillsdale, NJ: Lawrence Erlbaum.

Brantlinger, E. (2003). *Dividing classes: How the middle class negotiates and rationalizes school advantage*. New York, NY: Routledge Falmer.

Briggs, K., Cheney, G. R., Davis, J., & Moll, K. (2013). *Operating in the dark: What outdated state policies and data gaps mean for effective school leadership*. Dallas, TX: George W. Bush Institute.

Broad Foundation & Thomas B. Fordham Institute. (2003). *Better leaders for America's schools: A manifesto*. Retrieved from www.ed excellencemedia.net/publications/2003/200305_betterleaders/manifesto.pdf

Brown, K. (2005). Pivotal points: History, development, and promise of the principalship. In F. English (Ed.), *The SAGE handbook of educational leadership: Advances in theory, research, and practice* (pp. 109–141). Thousand Oaks, CA: SAGE.

Brundrett, M. (2001). The development of school leadership preparation programmes in England and the USA. *Educational Management and Administration, 29*(2), 229–245.

Buchmann, C., & Hannum, E. (2001). Education and stratification in developing countries: A review of theories and research. *Annual Review of Sociology, 27*, 77–102.

Bumiller, E. (2008, January 30). Research groups boom in Washington. *New York Times*, p. A12.

Calhoun, C. (1995). Habitus, field and capital: The question of historical specificity. In C. Calhoun, E.

LiPuma, & M. Postone (Eds.), *Bourdieu: Critical perspectives* (pp. 61–88). Oxford, UK: Blackwell.

Carnevale, A. P. (2012, July 6). The great sorting. *Chronicle of Higher Education*, p. B8. Retrieved from http://chronicle.com/article/The-Great-Sorting/132635/

Cherryholmes, C. (1988). *Power and criticism: Poststructural investigations in education*. New York, NY: Teachers College Press.

Chiu, M. M. (2007). Families, economics, cultures and science achievement in 41 countries: Country-, school-, and student-level analyses. *Journal of Family Psychology, 21*, 510–519.

Chiu, M. M., & Khoo, I. (2005). Effects of school population socioeconomic status on individual academic achievement. *Journal of Educational Research, 42*(4), 575–603.

Chudgar, A., & Luschei, T. F. (2009, September). National income, income inequality, and the importance of schools: A hierarchical cross-national comparison. *American Educational Research Journal, 46*(3), 626–658.

Coleman, J. (1961). *The adolescent society: The social life of the teenager and its impact on education*. New York, NY: Free Press.

Collins, G. (2012, June 12). How Texas inflicts bad textbooks on us. *New York Review of Books, 59*(11), 18–20.

Collins, P. (2013, December 20). A History Boys education is not for everyone. *London Times*, p. 17.

Collins, R. (1998). *The sociology of philosophies: A global theory of intellectual change*. Cambridge, MA: Belknap Press of Harvard University Press.

Condron, D. J. (2011, March). Egalitarianism and educational excellence: Compatible goals for affluent societies? *Educational Researcher, 40*(2), 47–55.

Council of Chief State School Officers. (2008). *Educational leadership policy standards*. Washington, DC: Author. Retrieved from http://www.ccsso.org/Documents/2008/Educational_Leadership_Policy_Standards_2008.pdf

Culbertson, J. (1988). A century's quest for a knowledge base. In N. J. Boyan (Ed.), *Handbook of research on educational administration* (pp. 3–26). New York, NY: Longman.

daCosta, G. A. (1978). Orphans and outlaws: Some impacts of racism. *Multiculturalism, 2*(1), 4–7.

Davis, M. R. (2013, April 24). Education industry players exert public-policy influence. *Education Week, 32*(29), 52–53.

Dillon, S. (2011, May 22). Gates spending big to influence education. *News & Observer*, pp. 1A, 11A.

Dimaggio, P. (1982, April). Cultural capital and social success. *American Sociological Review, 47*, 189–201.

Dumais, S. A. (2006). Early childhood cultural capital, parental habitus, and teachers' perceptions. *Poetics, 34*, 83–107.

Dyer, R. (1997). *White: Essays on race and culture*. New York, NY: Routledge.

Educational Testing Service. (1997). *School leaders licensure assessment: Candidate information bulletin*. Princeton, NJ: Author.

Eisner, E. (1992). Curriculum ideologies. In P. W. Jackson (Ed.),

Handbook of research on curriculum (pp. 302–326). New York, NY: Macmillan.

Emery, K., & Ohanian, S. (2004). *Why is corporate America bashing our public schools?* Portsmouth, NH: Heinemann.

English, F. W. (2000). Psst! What does one call a set of non-empirical beliefs required to be accepted on faith and enforced by authority? [Answer: A Religion, aka the ISLLC Standards]. *International Journal of Leadership in Education: Theory and Practice, 3*(2), 159–167.

English, F. W. (2003). Cookie-cutter leaders for cookie-cutter schools: The teleology of standardization and the de-legitimation of the university in educational leadership preparation. *Leadership and Policy in Schools, 2*(1), 27–46.

English, F. W. (2006). The unintended consequences of a standardized knowledge base in advancing educational leadership preparation. *Educational Administration Quarterly, 42*(3), 461–472.

English, F. W. (2010). *Deciding what to teach and test* (3rd ed.). Thousand Oaks, CA: Corwin.

English, F. W. (2014). *Educational leadership in the age of greed.* Ypsilanti, MI: NCPEA Press.

English, F. W., & Crowder, Z. (2013, May). *Counterspin: A discourse analysis of Eli Broad's leadership brag sheet.* Paper presented at the annual conference of the American Educational Research Association, San Francisco, California.

English, F. W., & Papa, R. (2010). *Restoring human agency to educational administration.* Lancaster, PA: Proactive.

Fergus, E., & Noguera, P. (2010). Doing what it takes to prepare Black and Latino males in college. In C. Edley & J. Ruiz (Eds.), *Changing places: How communities will improve the health of boys of color* (pp. 97–139). Berkeley: University of California Press.

Finn, C. (1991). *We must take charge.* New York, NY: Basic Books.

Flanary, R. (2010, August). Verbal report. NCPEA Executive Board meeting, Washington, D.C.

Fordham, S., & Ogbu, J. (1986). Black students' school success: Coping with the "burden of 'acting white.'" *Urban Review, 18*(3), 176–206.

Foucault, M. (1974). *The archaeology of knowledge.* London: Tavistock.

Foucault, M. (1979). *Discipline and punish: The birth of the prison.* New York, NY: Random House.

Frank, T. (2010, March 17). Don't mess with the Texas board of ed. *Wall Street Journal*, p. A19.

Gans, H. J. (1972). Foreword. In C. Greer, *The Great School Legend: A revisionist interpretation of American public education* (pp. vii–xiii). New York, NY: Basic Books.

Gass, J., & Chieppo, C. (2013, May 28). Common Core education is uncommonly inadequate. *Wall Street Journal*, p. A15.

Gewertz, C. (2012, September 19). Two versions of 'common' test eyed. *Education Week, 32*(4), 1, 19.

Gilmartin, S. K., Li, E., & Aschbacher, O. (2006). The relationship between interest in physical science/engineering, science class experiences, and family contexts: Variations by gender and race/ethnicity among secondary students. *Journal of*

Women and Minorities in Science and Engineering, 12(2–3), 179–207.

Giroux, H. (2004). *The terror of neoliberalism: Authoritarianism and the eclipse of democracy.* Boulder, CO: Paradigm.

Grady, R. E. (2013, December 23). Obama's misguided obsession with inequality. *Wall Street Journal*, p. A15.

Grant, G. (1988). *The world we created at Hamilton High.* Cambridge, MA: Harvard University Press.

Greer, C. (1972). *The great school legend: A revisionist interpretation of American public education.* New York, NY: Basic Books.

Grenfell, M. (2004). *Pierre Bourdieu: Agent provocateur.* London: Continuum.

Grenfell, M. (2007). *Pierre Bourdieu: Education and training.* London: Continuum.

Griffiths, D., Stout, R., & Forsyth, P. (1988). *Leaders for America's schools: The report and papers of the National Commission on Excellence in Educational Administration.* Berkeley, CA: McCutchan.

Groopman, J. (2007). *How doctors think.* Boston, MA: Houghton Mifflin.

Groopman, J. (2010). Health care: Who knows best? *New York Review of Books, 43*(2), 12–15.

Gunter, H. (2002a). *Leaders and leadership in education.* London: Paul Chapman.

Gunter, H. (2002b). Purposes and positions in the field of education management. *Educational Management and Administration, 30*(1), 7–26.

Gunter, H. (2006). Knowledge production in the field of educational leadership: A place for intellectual histories. *Journal of Educational Administration and History, 38*(2), 201–216.

Gunter, H., & Thompson, P. (2010). Life on Mars: Headteachers before the national college. *Journal of Educational Administration and History, 42*(3), 203–222.

Gurwitz, J. (2010, March 21). SBOE curriculum changes are not true conservatism. *San Antonio Light*, p. 9B.

Hall, E. T. (1966). *The silent language.* New York, NY: Doubleday.

Hanushek, E. A., & Luque, J. A. (2003). Efficiency and equity in schools around the world. *Economics of Education Review, 22*, 481–502.

Harris, K. (1982). *Teachers and classes: A Marxist analysis.* London: Routledge & Kegan Paul.

Harvey, D. (2005). *A brief history of neoliberalism.* Oxford, UK: Oxford University Press.

Hechinger, J. (2007, September 26). School kids post modest gains in national test. *Wall Street Journal*, p. D1.

Heitin, L. (2012, August 29). Gallup poll: Student success linked to positive outlook. *Education Week, 32*(2), 11.

Hess, F. (2003, July 9). A license to lead? *Education Week, 22*(42), 39.

Hess, F., & Kelly, A. P. (2005, May 18). Learning to lead? *Education Week, 24*(37), 44.

Hessel, K., & Holloway, J. (2002). *A framework for school leaders: Linking the ISLLC Standards to practice.* Princeton, NJ: Educational Testing Service.

Heymann, J. (2002). *Can working families ever win?* (J. Cohen & J. Rogers, Eds.). Boston, MA: Beacon Press.

Higgleton, E., Sargeant, H., & Seaton, A. (1999). *Chambers pocket dictionary*. Glasgow, UK: Chambers Harrap.

Honneth, A., Kocyba, H., & Schwibs, B. (1986). The struggle for symbolic order: An interview with Pierre Bourdieu. *Theory, Culture and Society, 3*, 35–51.

Hungary's Roma: How to get out of a vicious circle. (2013, August 10). *The Economist*, 47.

Irvin, G. (2008). *Super rich: The rise of inequality in Britain and the United States*. Malden, MA: Polity Press.

Jencks, C., Smith, M., Acland, H., Bane, M. J., Cohen, D., Gintis, H., . . . Michelson, S. (1972). *Inequality: A reassessment of the effect of family and schooling in America*. New York, NY: Basic Books.

Jenkins, R. (2002). *Pierre Bourdieu* (Rev. ed.). London: Routledge.

Jobrack, B. (2012, August 8). Solving the textbook–Common Core conundrum. *Education Week, 31*(37), 36, 30.

Johnson, R. (1993). Editor's introduction: Pierre Bourdieu on art, literature and culture. In P. Bourdieu, *The field of cultural production* (pp. 1–28). New York, NY: Columbia University.

Jordan, M. (2012, June 18). Asians top immigration class. *Wall Street Journal*. Retrieved from http://online.wsj.com/news/articles/SB10001424052702303379204577474743811707050

Kahlenberg, R. D. (2012, July 6). Magnifying social inequality. *Chronicle of Higher Education*, p. B6. Retrieved from http://chronicle.com/article/Magnifying-Social-Inequality/132627/

Kanigel, R. (1997). *The one best way: Frederick Winslow Taylor and the enigma of efficiency*. New York, NY: Viking Penguin.

Katz, M. (1968). *The irony of early school reform: Educational innovation in mid-nineteenth century Massachusetts*. Boston, MA: Beacon Press.

Khurana, R. (2002). *Search for a corporate savior: The irrational quest for charismatic CEOs*. Princeton, NJ: Princeton University Press.

Kuhn, T. (1996). *The structure of scientific revolutions*. Chicago, IL: University of Chicago Press.

Kumashiro, K. K. (2008). *The seduction of common sense: How the right has framed the debate on America's schools*. New York, NY: Teachers College Press.

Labaree, D. F. (1988). *The making of an American high school: The credentials market and the Central High School of Philadelphia, 1838–1939*. New Haven, CT: Yale University Press.

Lagasse, P. (Ed.). (1994). Algeria. In *Columbia Encyclopedia* (3rd ed., p. 21). New York, NY: Columbia University Press.

Lakatos, I. (1999). Lectures on scientific method. In M. Motterlini (Ed.), *For and against method* (pp. 19–113). Chicago, IL: University of Chicago Press.

Lamont, M., & Lareau, A. (1988). Cultural capital: Allusions, gaps, and glissandos in recent theoretical developments. *Sociological Theory, 6*(2), 153–168.

Lane, J. F. (2006). *Bourdieu's politics: Problems and possibilities*. London: Routledge.

Lareau, A. (2011). *Unequal childhoods: Class, race and family life*. Berkeley: University of California Press.

Lebaron, F. (2010). Bourdieu in a multi-dimensional perspective. In E. Silva & A. Warde (Eds.), *Cultural analysis and Bourdieu's legacy* (pp. 142–150). London: Routledge.

Leonardo, Z. (2007). The war on schools: NCLB, nation creation and the educational construction of whiteness. *Race, Ethnicity and Education, 10*(3), 261–278.

Levinson, M. P. (2007). Literacy in English Gypsy communities: Cultural capital manifested as negative assets. American Educational Research Journal, 44(1), 5–39.

LiPuma, E. (1993). Culture and the concept of culture in a theory of practice. In C. Calhoun, E. LiPuma, & M. Postone (Eds.), *Bourdieu: Critical perspectives* (pp. 14–34). Chicago, IL: University of Chicago Press.

Lloyd, S. C. (2012, June 1). As new federal rules kick in on graduation rates, states change their calculations. *Education Week, 31*(35), 32.

Losing her stripes? Tiger mothers in Singapore. (2012, September 22). *The Economist*, 49.

Lucas, S. R. (1999). *Tracking inequality: Stratification and mobility in American high schools*. New York, NY: Teachers College Press.

Lumby, J., & English, F. W. (2009). From simplicism to complexity in leadership identity and preparation: Exploring the lineage and dark secrets. *International Journal of Leadership in Education, 12*(2), 95–114.

MacLeod, J. (1987). *Ain't no makin' it: Leveled aspirations in a low-income neighborhood*. Boulder, CO: Westview Press.

Maddern, K. (2012, June 22). The road less travelled. *Think, Educate, Share*, 28–32. Retrieved from http://www.tes.co.uk/article.aspx?storycode=6257857

Maton, K. (2010). Habitus. In M. Grenfell (Ed.), *Pierre Bourdieu: Key concepts* (pp. 49–65). Durham, UK: Acumen.

Maxwell, L. A. (2006, December 20). Finn basks in role as standards-bearer, gadfly. *Education Week, 26*(16), 1, 16.

Maxwell, L. A. (2012, August 29). African-American males in policy spotlight: Low achievement, high dropout rates a persistent problem. *Education Week, 32*, 9.

Maynor, P. (2011). *Bourdieu's habitus and the educational achievement of North Carolina's American Indian students: An empirical investigation*. Unpublished doctoral dissertation, University of North Carolina at Chapel Hill.

McCarthy, M. (1999). The evolution of educational leadership preparation programs. In J. Murphy & K. S. Louis (Eds.), *Handbook of research on educational administration* (2nd ed., pp. 119–140). San Francisco, CA: Jossey-Bass.

McDonnell, L. M., & Weatherford, M. S. (2013, December). Organized interests and the Common Core. *Educational Researcher, 42*(9), 488–497.

Medina, M. (1988). Hispanic apartheid in American public education. *Educational Administration Quarterly, 24*, 336–349.

Meyers, E., & Rust, F. (2000, May 31). The test doesn't tell all. *Education Week, 19*(38), 34, 37.

Mullen, C., Samier, E., Brindley, S., English, F., & Carr, N. (2013). An epistemic frame analysis of neo-liberal culture and politics in the US, UK, and the UAE. *Interchange, 43*(3), 187–228.

Murphy, J. (1999). New consumerism: Evolving market dynamics in the institutional dimension of schooling. In J. Murphy & K. S. Louis (Eds.), *Handbook of research on educational administration* (pp. 405–420). San Francisco, CA: Jossey-Bass.

Murphy, J. (2005). Unpacking the foundations of the ISLLC standards and addressing concerns in the academic community. *Educational Administration Quarterly, 41*(1), 154–191.

Murphy, J., Yff, J., & Shipman, N. (2000). Implementation of the interstate school leaders licensure consortium standards. *International Journal of Leadership in Education: Theory and Practice, 3*(1), 17–40.

Nash, G. B., Crabtree, C., & Dunn, R. E. (1997). *History on trial.* New York, NY: Alfred A. Knopf.

Oakes, J. (1985). *Keeping track: How schools structure inequality.* New Haven, CT: Yale University Press.

Parenti, M. (1978). *Power and the powerless.* New York, NY: St. Martin's Press.

Paton, G. (2012, January 31). Thousands of 'dead end' courses axed from school tables. *Telegraph.* Retrieved from http://www.telegraph.co.uk/education/educationnews/9050009/Thousands-of-dead-end-courses-axed-from-school-tables.html

Paton, G. (2013, June 17). Universities must recruit 3,700 more state school students. *Telegraph.* Retrieved from http://www.telegraph.co.uk/education/educationnews/10121834/Universities-must-recruit-3700-more-state-school-students.html

Portes, A. (1998). Social capital: Its origin and applications in modern sociology. *Annual Review of Sociology, 24,* 1–24.

Power, S., Edwards, T., Whitty, G., & Wigfall, V. (2003). *Education and the middle class.* Philadelphia, PA: Open University Press.

Prier, D. D. (2012). *Culturally relevant teaching: Hip-Hop pedagogy in urban schools.* New York, NY: Peter Lang.

Ravitch, D. (2010a). *The life and death of the great American school system: How testing and choice are undermining education.* New York, NY: Basic Books.

Ravitch, D. (2010b, March 9). Why I changed my mind about school reform. *Wall Street Journal,* p. A21.

Ravitch, D. (2012). *Reign of error: The hoax of the privatization movement and the danger to America's public schools.* New York, NY: Alfred A. Knopf.

Ream, R. K., & Palardy, G. J. (2008, June). Re-examining social class differences in the availability and the educational utility of parental social capital. *American Educational Research Journal, 45*(21), 238–273.

Reay, D. (2004). "It's all becoming a habitus": Beyond the habitual use of habitus in educational research. *British Journal of Sociology of Education, 25*(4), 431–444.

Reimer, E. W. (1971). *School is dead: An essay on alternatives in education.* New York, NY: Doubleday.

Riley, J. L. (2011, July 23–24). Was the $5 billion worth it? *Wall Street Journal*, p. A11.

Robson, K. (2009). Teenage time use as investment in cultural capital. In K. Robson & C. Sanders (Eds.), *Quantifying theory: Pierre Bourdieu* (pp. 105–116). New York, NY: Springer.

Rohlen, T. P. (1983). *Japan's high schools*. Berkeley: University of California Press.

Rotberg, I. C. (2011, September 14). International test scores, irrelevant policies: Misleading rhetoric overlooks poverty's impact. *Education Week, 31*(3), 32.

Rothman, R. (2011). *Something in common: The Common Core standards and the next chapter in American education*. Cambridge, MA: Harvard University Press.

Rothstein, R. (2004). *Class and schools: Using social, economic, and educational reform to close the Black–White achievement gap*. New York, NY: Teachers College Press.

Sahlberg, P. (2011). *Finnish lessons: What can the world learn from educational change in Finland?* New York, NY: Teachers College Press.

Sapon-Shevin, M. (1994). *Playing favorites: Gifted education and the disruption of community*. Albany: SUNY Press.

Savage, L., & English, F. (2013). Unmasking social injustice in the classroom: The achievement gap and Bourdieu's cultural reproduction theory. In S. Harris & S. Edmonson (Eds.), *Critical social justice issues for school practitioners* (pp. 121–145). Ypsilanti, MI: NCPEA Publications.

Sawchuk, S. (2012, May 16). New breed of advocacy groups shakes up education field. *Education Week, 31*(31), 1, 19.

Schneider, J., & Fede, H. (2002, March 28). *What distinguishes nationally recognized educational administration departments?* [PowerPoint presentation]. Arlington, VA: American Association of School Administrators.

Schott Foundation. (2010). *Yes we can: The 2010 Schott 50 state report on public education of black males*. Cambridge, MA: Author.

Schubert, J. D. (2008). Suffering. In M. Grenfell (Ed.), *Pierre Bourdieu: Key concepts* (pp. 183–189). Durham, UK: Acumen.

Shah, N., & Maxwell, L. A. (2012, August 22). Study: Schools suspend Black students three times more often than whites. *Education Week, 32*(1), 6.

Shannon, K. (2012, September 26). Researchers say nation's schools undergo more resegregation. *Education Week, 32*(5), 5.

Shaw, D. (2013, December 18). State grammar schools and social mobility. *The Times*, p. 21.

Shipman, N. J. (2006). Interstate School Leaders Licensure Consortium. In F. English (Ed.), *Encyclopedia of educational leadership and administration* (pp. 524–526). Thousand Oaks, CA: SAGE.

Shipman, N. J., Queen, J. A., & Peel, H. A. (2007). *Transforming school leadership with ISLLC and ELCC*. Larchmont, NY: Eye on Education.

Shor, I. (1986). *Culture wars: School and society in the conservative restoration 1969–1984*. Boston, MA: Routledge & Kegan Paul.

Smith, E. (2013, April 29). 'No child left behind' gets left behind. *Wall Street Journal*, p. A17.

Smith, H. (2012). *Who stole the American dream?* New York, NY: Random House.

Smith, M. L., Heinscke, W., & Jarvis, P. F. (2004). *Political spectacle and the fate of American schools.* New York, NY: Routledge Falmer.

Solomon, R. (1992). *Black resistance in high school: Forging a separatist culture.* Albany: SUNY Press.

Southern Regional Education Board. (2006). *Schools can't wait: Accelerating the redesign of university principal preparation programs.* Atlanta, GA: Author.

Sparks, S. D. (2011, July 13). 20-Year Hispanic academic gaps persist in math, reading. *Education Week, 30*(36), 14.

Stevens, L. (2010, April 3–4). Merkel, Erdoğan spar over schools, spotlighting Turks' role in Germany. *Wall Street Journal*, p. A9.

Stewart, E. B., Stewart, E. A., & Simons, R. L. (2007). The effect of neighborhood context on the college aspirations of African American adolescents. *American Educational Research Journal, 44*(4), 896–919.

Swalwell, K., & Sherman, W. (2012, Fall). Confronting white privilege. *Teaching Tolerance, 42,* 23–26.

Swartz, D. (1997). *Culture and power: The sociology of Pierre Bourdieu.* Chicago, IL: University of Chicago Press.

Swartz, D. (2010). Pierre Bourdieu's political sociology and public sociology. In E. Silva & A. Warde (Eds.), *Cultural analysis and Bourdieu's legacy: Setting accounts and developing alternatives* (pp. 45–60). London: Routledge.

Tallerico, M. (2006). Department of education. In F. English (Ed.), *Encyclopedia of educational leadership and administration* (pp. 280–281). Thousand Oaks, CA: SAGE.

Thompson, J. B. (1991). Editor's introduction. In P. Bourdieu, *Language and symbolic power* (pp. 1–31). Cambridge, MA: Harvard University Press.

Thompson, J. D. (1967). *Organizations in action.* New York, NY: McGraw-Hill.

Thomson, P. (2008). Headteacher critique and resistance: A challenge for policy, and for leadership/management scholars. *Journal of Educational Administration and History, 40*(2), 85–100.

Thomson, P. (2009). Field. In M. Grenfell (Ed.), *Pierre Bourdieu: Key concepts* (pp. 67–84). Durham, UK: Acumen.

Tinker, tailor, glass-eye-maker. (2011, February 5). *The Economist,* 84.

Tracy, T. (2012, March 12). School standards wade into climate debate. *Wall Street Journal*, p. A6.

Turney-Purta, J., Lehman, R., Oswald, H., & Schulz, W. (2001). *Citizenship and education in twenty-eight countries: Civic knowledge and engagement at age fourteen.* Amsterdam, Netherlands: International Association for the Evaluation of Educational Achievement.

Vasagar, J. (2012, January 30). Thousands of vocational qualifications to be stripped out of GCSE league tables. *Guardian.* Retrieved from http://www.theguardian.com/education/2012/jan/31/

vocational-qualifications-stripped-league-tables

Wacquant, L. J. D. (1992). Toward a social praxeology: The structure and logic of Bourdieu's sociology. In P. Bourdieu & L. J. D. Wacquant, *An invitation to reflexive sociology* (pp. 1–59). Chicago, IL: University of Chicago Press.

Webb, J., Schirato, T., & Danaher, G. (2002). *Understanding Bourdieu.* London: SAGE.

Willis, P. (1977). *Learning to labor: How working class kids get working class jobs.* New York, NY: Columbia University Press.

Wilson, W. J. (1987). *The truly disadvantaged.* Chicago, IL: University of Chicago Press.

Wilson, W. J. (1996). *When work disappears: The world of the new urban poor.* New York, NY: Vintage.

Winfield, A. G. (2012). Resuscitating bad science: Eugenics past and present. In W. H. Watkins (Ed.), *The assault on public education* (pp. 143–159). New York, NY: Teachers College Press.

Wolf, A. (2011). *Review of vocational education: The Wolf report.* Retrieved from https://www.gov.uk/government/uploads/system/uploads/attachment_data/file/180504/DFE-00031-2011.pdf

Yalom, M. (2004). *Birth of the chess queen.* New York, NY: Harper Collins.

Index

academic credentials, 53, 65
academic failure, 64
academic qualifications, 33
 see also Cheryl Bolton
achievement gap, between racial
 groups, 54
African-Americans, 29, 38
Alinsky, S., 40
American Association of School
 Administrators (AASA), 86
American Educational Research
 Association (AERA), 86
American Enterprise Institute, 9, 85
 see Frederick Hess
Anderson, G., 40, 85, 91
Apple, M., 45, 85
Archer, L., 30, 47
Asians, in the United States, 47
Association for Supervision and
 Curriculum Development
 (ASCD), 86

Banchero, S., 37
Berger, J., 35
best practices, as misconceived, 96
billionaire boys club, 85
 see also Diane Ravitch
Black males, 22, 38
Blackmore, J., 85, 110
Blau, P., 41
Bolton, C., 19, 33–34, 109
Bourdieu, P.,
 Algerian experience, 4–5
 biography of, 3–6
 lack of cultural capital as a child,
  57–58

pursuit of reality, 21
relational field of educational
 interests, 10
unique vocabulary of academic
 writing, 1, 7–8
Bowles, S., 17, 31, 49, 68
Boykin, A., 36
Brantlinger, E., 25, 40, 44
Brian, B., 27
Brindley, S., 20
Broad, E., 9, 85, 90, 104
Broad Superintendents Academy, 90
Brown, K., 81
Business Roundtable, 61

capital, three forms of, 55–62, 71
Center for European Sociology, 6
Central High School, of
 Philadelphia, 63
 see also David Labaree
charisma ideology, 90
 see also Rakesh Khurana
Cherryholmes, C., 35
children, of racial minorities in
 schools, 36
class, Marxian view of and critique
 by Bourdieu, 17, 31–32
climate change, 11
Coleman, J., 16
collective habitus, 31
Collins, R., 6
common core curriculum standards
 in the U.S., 13, 26, 35, 52, 61, 73,
 85, 91, 106
Condron, D., 3, 17
Congress of the United States, 11

core technologies, 84, 92, 95
    see also Joseph Murphy
Council of Chief State School Officers
    (CCSSO), 61, 86
Crowder, Z., 91
Culbertson, J., 84
cultural arbitrary, 26, 35–36, 48,
    51, 106
cultural capital, 11, 57, 74
culture wars, 10
curriculum, content of, 53–54
    as a form of symbolic and cultural
        capital, 54
    as hidden, 67, 76
cycle of poverty, 29

Danaher, G., 19, 65
Darwin, C., 10
determinism, criticism of Bourdieu
    and habitus, 18, 31
domination, concept of, 23
doxa, doxic attitude, 19–20, 23, 42
Dyer, R., 45

economic capital, 56, 75
educational goals, 2
Eisner, E., 67, 76
Emery, K., 66, 92
English, F., 20, 24–25, 78, 80,
    84–85
Erdoğan, Recep Tayyip, of Turkey, 18

family structure, 46
Fergus, E., 22,38
field, concept of, 32–33, 50, 60
field, of power, 80, 86, 100
Finn, C., 85, 92
    see also Thomas B. Fordham Institute
Flanary, R., 20
Forsyth, P., 93
Foucault, M., 79, 81
    see also power-knowledge

Gallup poll, 64
Gates, B., 9, 85, 104
George W. Bush Foundation, of
    Texas, 89
Gintis, H., 17, 31, 49, 68

Giroux, H., 80
Gove, M., 12, 69
graduation rates of high schools in
    the United States, 44
Grant, G., 16
Greer, C., 15–16
Grenfell, M., xii, 4, 5, 6, 23
Griffiths, D., 93
Groopman, J., 96
Gueroult, M., 19
Gunter, H., 78–84
gypsy children, problems of, in
    school, 36–39
gypsy families, 47

habitus, concept of, 28, 50
habitus, durable, 42
habitus, in a neighborhood, 29
habitus, scholastic, 59
Hall, E., 35
Hamilton High School, in
    Philadelphia, 16
    see also Gerald Grant
hegemony, of a field, 9
Heritage Foundation, 9
Hess, F., 85, 90
    see also American Enterprise Institute
Hessel, K., 82
history curriculum, controversy
    regarding, 11–12
Holloway, J., 82
home environment, 46
human perception, 35
Hunt, J.G., 61
Hunt Institute, of North Carolina, 61

illusio, concept of, 42–43, 52
India, Right to Education Act, 16
inequality, legitimization of, by
    schools, 15, 45
International Association for the
    Evaluation of Educational
    Achievement, 41
Interstate School Leaders Licensure
    Consortium (ISLLC), 81, 93, 96

Jackson, J., 38
Japanese high schools, 16

Jencks, C., 13
Jenkins, R., xii, 8, 18, 51–52
job standardization, 95

Katz, M., 14
Khurana, R., 90
knowledge claims, 79, 92
Kuhn, T., 19
Kumashiro, K., 15, 48, 85, 92
Labaree, D., 63
Lakatos, I., 93
Lane, J., 2, 20–21
Lareau, A., 15
leaders, codification of, 96
leadership standards, 24, 78
leadership, the deprofessionalization
    of, 78
left hand, of the state, 20, 103
legitimacy, in a field, 9, 97
life chances, 44, 53
linguistic capital, 13
LiPuma, E., 51, 74, 97
logic of work or practice, 40

Macleod, J., 36, 57
McCarthy, M., 85, 93
maldistribution of opportunity, 70–71
managerialism, concept of, 80, 100
marketizaton, of education, 107
Marxists, 20
Maton, K., 50
Maynor, P., 39
Merkel, A., 18
metanarrative, 35
metanoia, concept of, xii, 19
misrecognition, concept of, 14–18,
    24, 34
Mullen, C., 20
Murphy, J., 84–85, 94–95

Nash, G., 11
National Association of Secondary
    School Principals (NASSP), 85
National Association of School
    Superintendents, (the AASA), 85
National Association of State Boards
    of Education, 61
National Center for Science
    Education, 11

National Commission on
    Excellence in Educational
    Administration, 93
National Council for the
    Accreditation of Teacher
    Education (NCATE), 85
National Council of Professors of
    Educational Administration
    (NCPEA), 87
National Elementary School
    Principals Association, 85
National Governors
    Association, 61
National Professional Qualifications
    for Headteachers, 81
National Research Council, 11
neoliberalism, 110
neoliberals, 20, 84, 103
No Child Left Behind, 15, 26, 46
Noguera, P., 22, 38

Oakes, J., 47
Obama, B., 99
Ogbu, J., 48
Ohanian, S., 66, 92

Papa, R., 96
paradigm, 19
Parenti, M., 40
Parliament, of the United
    Kingdom, 11
Passeron, J., 6, 9, 13, 36, 39, 45, 51, 59,
    62, 70
pedagogic actions, 9
pedagogic authority, 9
pedagogic work, 8
pedagogy, definition of, 9
Peel, H., 26
Piatt, W., 64
Pini, M., 40, 85, 91
power, in symbolic form, 60
power knowledge, concept of, 79
    see also Michel Foucault
Prier, D., 15, 27, 36, 46

Queen, Allen, J., 26

Race to the Top, 9, 26, 46, 61
rationality, technical, 84

Ravitch, D., 9, 27, 40, 85, 89
  see also billionaire boys club
reality, as multiperspectival, 35
reflexive thinking, 19
regime of truth, concept of, 79
Reimer, E., 12, 27
right hand, of the state, 20, 103
Rohlen, T., 16
Roma children, problems of, in
  school, 36–39
Rothman, R., 61
Rothstein, R., 41
rules of the game, concept of, 50

Sahlberg, P., 3, 17
Samier, E., 20
Sapon-Shevin, M., 40
Sartre, J. P., 6
Savage, L., 3, 25
Schirato, T., 1, 9, 65
scholasticism, in regards to
  leadership standards, 96
schools, as a form of cultural capital,
  58, 65
school failure, by race, 23
school practitioners, 22
Schott Foundation, 38
Scott, W. R., 41
Schubert, J. D., 75
Shipman, N., 26, 82, 85, 94
Shor, I., 10
Smith, E., 15
Smith, H., 39
social agents, 60
social capital, 56, 75
social hierarchies, 60
social justice, 92, 99, 103, 110
social space, 1, 32, 72
Solomon, R. P., 36, 48
Southern Regional Education Board, 80
standardization, 95
Stout, R., 90
structure, concept of, 28
Swartz, D., 20, 34, 50, 56, 70
symbolic capital, 56, 61
symbolic power, 62, 73

Tallerico, M., 85
Taylor, F., 100
Teach for America, 91
test scores, 54
Texas State Board of Education, 62
the normalizing gaze, 81
  see also Michel Foucault
The Wolf Report, 69
the performing school, in the
  UK, 81
theory of evolution, 10–11
Thomas B. Fordham Institute, 85
  See also Chester Finn
Thompson, J. D., 84
Thompson, P., 51, 71
tiger moms, Asian, 47
truth, as a system of ordered
  procedures, 79

United States Chamber of
  Commerce, 106
University Council for Educational
  Administration (UCEA),
  87, 93
United States Department of
  Education, 9
  Office for Civil Rights, 38
United States Supreme Court, 37

vielseitigkeit, 7
violence, in symbolic form of,
  59–60, 75
vision, of leaders, 83
vocational education, 68
voucher plans, 98

Wacquant, L., 32, 34, 51,
  75, 100
wealth gap, 16
Webb, J., 19, 65
Weber, M., 7
white privilege, concept of, 45
Winfield, A., 38
Wolf, A., 69
  see also The Wolf Report
Yalom, M., 51

⑨SAGE research**methods**

The essential online tool for researchers from the
world's leading methods publisher

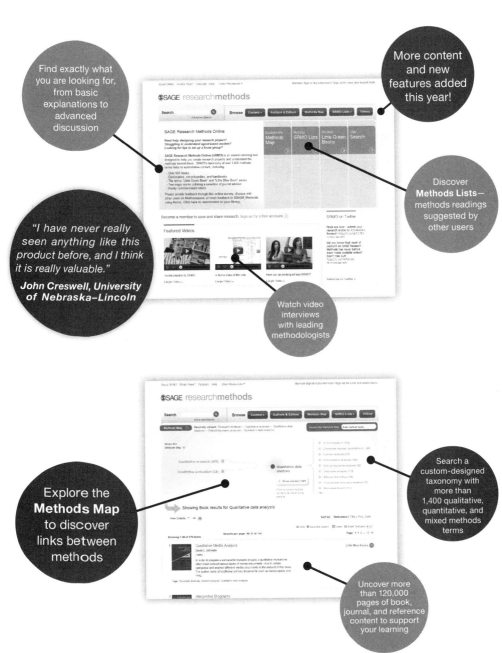

Find exactly what
you are looking for,
from basic
explanations to
advanced
discussion

More content
and new
features added
this year!

Discover
Methods Lists—
methods readings
suggested by
other users

"*I have never really
seen anything like this
product before, and I think
it is really valuable.*"
**John Creswell, University
of Nebraska–Lincoln**

Watch video
interviews
with leading
methodologists

Explore the
Methods Map
to discover
links between
methods

Search a
custom-designed
taxonomy with
more than
1,400 qualitative,
quantitative, and
mixed methods
terms

Uncover more
than 120,000
pages of book,
journal, and reference
content to support
your learning

Find out more at
www.sageresearchmethods.com